TOASTS
for all
Occasions

REVISED EDITION

By

Jeff & Deborah Herman

NEW PAGE BOOKS
A division of The Career Press, Inc.
Franklin Lakes, NJ

TOASTS FOR ALL OCCASIONS, REVISED EDITION
EDITED BY KATE HENCHES
TYPESET BY EILEEN DOW MUNSON
Cover design by Foster & Foster, Inc.
Printed in the U.S.A. by Book-mart Press

To order this title, please call toll-free 1-800-CAREER-1 (NJ and Canada: 201-848-0310) to order using VISA or MasterCard, or for further information on books from Career Press.

The Career Press, Inc., 3 Tice Road, PO Box 687,
Franklin Lakes, NJ 07417
www.careerpress.com
www.newpagebooks.com

Library of Congress Cataloging-in-Publication Data
available upon request.
ISBN 1-56414-709-6

We dedicate this book
to all those who know
how to embrace
the good things in life.

To., Dennis
Barnes

from Aunt Vera

2010 Xmas

Acknowledgments

So many of our favorite toasts were passed down from one happy reveler to another. We would love to acknowledge all of those gifted with the ability to create witticisms and sentimentalities special enough to be shared and concise enough to be remembered, so here is our general thank you. Thank you to those who have set up Internet chats or Websites featuring your special poems and toasts. We want this book to reflect the language of our times as well as tradition. What better way than to glean up-to-the-minute contributions through the benefit of modern technology?

We would like to thank all the members of the National Speakers Association who took time out of their busy schedules to make wonderful contributions of advice and special toasts to our "Favorite Toasts from Favorite Hosts" chapter. They are: Ralph Archbold, Patricia Ball, Janelle Barlow, Frank Basile, Sheila Murray Bethel, Doc Blakely, Dianna Booher, Dave Broadfoot, Marjorie Brody, Dr. Gayle Carson, Steve Chandler, John Crudele, John Patrick Dolan, Art Fettig, Joyce Gibb, Richard Hadden, Keith Harrell, Cher Holton, Shep Hyken, Doug Jones, Brian Lee, Florence Littauer, Dennis McQuistion, W. Mitchell, Dr. Terry Paulson, Chuck Reeves, David A. Rich, Tim Richardson, Lee Robert, Dick Semaan, Jim Tunney, Al Walker, Somers White, Mikki Williams, and Dave Yoho.

We will always miss our friend, the late Stanley Ralph Ross, writer-producer-director-actor (see him in *Babe 2: A Pig in the City*). He provided many memorable toasts, including the contributions from Frank Sinatra and Steve Allen.

Special thanks to NSA members and friends Danielle Kennedy and Jack Canfield, and to Michael Aun and Jeff Slutsky who shared toasts, advice, and excerpts from their wonderful book, *The International Toastmasters Guide to Successful Speaking* (Dearborn Trade Publishing, 1997).

Special, special thanks to Art Linkletter, a national treasure and a personal hero of Deborah's, who so graciously responded to our questionnaire in spite of his overwhelming commitments.

We greatly appreciate the efforts of the staff of Career Press for helping to develop this project.

We could not have written this book without the help of friends and family members who contributed favorite stories and toasts, some not suitable to print. We would like to thank our spouses—us—so we may as well acknowledge us with a toast:

> To a happy and wonderful life together filled
> with health and prosperity, which is what we
> wish for all of you.

Table of Contents

Introduction

When we began this project of compiling toasts for all occasions, we almost drove ourselves crazy looking for formal resources to provide us with definitive information on writing toasts and toast-giving. What we discovered was that toast-giving is a highly personal art. To give a toast is to honor someone you care about—or for whom you are publicly obligated to care. Whether at a wedding, birthday party, or gathering among friends, the right toast sets the mood for the evening's festivities and the memories to be taken from the moment.

A toast is the rare occasion when someone who could otherwise never say two words in front of a staring crowd is given the opportunity to take the spotlight. The good thing about a toast is that the spotlight may be on the toaster, but the attention should actually be paid to the toastee. If you are the type of person who freezes at the thought of being in front of a group of people and having to speak, this book will help you lighten up, enjoy yourself, and say something appropriate for the occasion.

As far as we can determine, toasts can be found as far back as this one, which was translated by Miguel Civil, of the Oriental Institute of the University of Chicago. According to studies, this is a 5,000-year-old toast that was given to a woman tavern keeper in ancient Mesopotamia:

> Let the heart of the gakko vat be our heart!
> What makes your heart feel wonderful,
> Makes also our heart feel wonderful.
> Our liver is happy, our heart is joyful.
> You poured a libation over the brick of destiny,
> You placed the foundations in peace and
> prosperity.

May Ninkasi live together with you!
Let her pour for you beer and wine,
Let the pouring of the sweet liquor resound
pleasantly for you!
In the reed buckets there is sweet beer,
I will make cupbearers,
boys, and brewers stand by,
While I turn around the abundance of beer,
While I feel wonderful, I feel wonderful,
Drinking beer in a blissful mood,
Drinking liquor, feeling exhilarated,
With joy in the heart and a happy liver—
While my heart full of joy,
And my happy liver I covered with a garment
fit for a queen!

   Although we are not completely convinced the Mesopotamians understood the consequences of a "happy liver," we know they understood how to join people together to honor someone important to them. There may be older toasts, but we are unable to locate one. Every known culture has had a tradition of celebration, so we feel it is safe to say that people were probably toasting to each other's health as far back as the lost city of Atlantis.

   This book begins with "Favorite Toasts from Favorite Hosts." We were fortunate to receive many contributions from members of the National Speakers Association (NSA), an organization intended to enhance the level of professionalism among speakers in this country. We are very fortunate to be affiliated with this organization, and to know many of its fine members. Not only have they shared their personal favorites, they have given advice that should help even the most nervous and inexperienced toasters. Remember, you want your toast to be a good experience for you as well as for the honoree. If you heed the sage advice of the NSA speakers, you may find yourself on the road to a new career. You would be amazed at what happens to people when you put a microphone in their hands.

The rest of the book is broken down into categories of toasts. Keep in mind that toasts often do not fit completely in one category or another. If you are looking for a toast for a particular occasion, you might want to look through all the chapters to find something you could modify to suit your needs. This is your chance to do something really original. For those few moments—and they should be brief—you can choose what to say and how to say it. We make no claims or representations that there won't be dire consequences if you say something tactless or inappropriate, but we can guarantee that originality and speaking from your heart are great places from which to begin.

Toasts are associated with joyous occasions. Humor, inspiration, and sentimentality are all welcome. Choose the type of toast that suits your personality most comfortably. If you can't find it here, make it up and let us know.

Chapter 1

Favorite Toasts from Favorite Hosts

T he National Speakers Association is an organization dedicated to advancing the art and value of experts who speak professionally. Although we have never heard the term "professional toast-giver," these members of the National Speakers Association can guarantee that when people need someone to give a toast, they are often first on the list. Not only have they graciously shared their favorite toasts, they have shared their sage advice as to the do's and don'ts for the would-be toast-giver.

Ralph Archbold, a professional speaker who often portrays the historical character Benjamin Franklin, offers this perspective:

"We used to toast once to each of our 13 states. Now that we have 50, it could make for an interesting evening! I like one that says:

> Perpetual itching
> without benefit of scratching,
> to all of your enemies.

"When giving a toast, make it short, make it pertain to the occasion and the people involved, and raise your glass high."

Patricia Ball, author of *Straight Talk Is More Than Words* (Trudy Knox Pub, 1996), shares this story:

"Mark Twain's *Diary of Adam and Eve* is part of the repertoire of memorable characters that I portray. At Eve's grave, Adam says, 'Wherever [Eve] was, there was Eden.' Upon the marriage of two close friends, I toasted the couple by telling the above story and then saying, 'Wherever they go, there is Eden.' "

Joyce Gibb, author and visionary:

Pay no attention to what critics say. There has never been set up a statue in honor of a critic.

Michael Aun is the 1978 Toastmasters International World Champion Speaker, and author of four books, including *The International Toastmaster's Guide to Successful Speaking*, *The Great Communicators*, *Marketing Masters*, and *Build a Better You, Starting Now!* He offers several toasts.

I could wish you good health,
I could wish you great wealth;
But your health could fail tomorrow,
And great wealth could bring deep sorrow.
So, I'll simply say, may God bless you!

Far better is to dare mighty things, to win
glorious triumphs, even though checkered by
failure, than to take rank with those poor spirits
who neither enjoy much nor suffer much, for
they live in a gray twilight that knows not
victory nor defeat.

—Theodore Roosevelt

Do all the good you can, by all the means you
can, in all the ways you can, in all the places
you can, to all the people you can, as long as
you can.

—John Wesley, English theologian

Do more than exist, live.
Do more than touch, feel.
Do more than look, observe.
Do more than read, absorb.
Do more than hear, listen.
Do more than think, ponder.
Do more than talk, say something.

"Have a list of books, such as *The Toastmaster's Guide to Successful Speaking* on a suggested reading list. Be reasonable—in time, content, appropriateness, and humor. Nobody likes a bore. Say it quick and sit down. Two good things will happen: You'll keep it short, and they won't get bored. Both of these should yield excellent results for you."

Janelle Barlow, co-author of *A Complaint is a Gift: Using Customer Feedback as a Strategic Tool*, says,

"I love toasts that let the audience learn something new about the person; and that gives better understanding of the celebrated person. Toast time is not complaint time—even if I believe complaints can be gifts. Toasts are a time for humor, praise, and congratulations."

Sheila Murray Bethel, author of the best-selling book, *Making a Difference: 12 Qualities that Make You a Leader* (Berkley Publishing Group, 1990), often uses a favorite Irish toast to honor friends:

May you live as long as you want, but never want
as long as you live.

"Do some research for a timely and appropriate toast. They can be great."

Frank Basile, professional speaker, author, and business executive, offers one of his favorites—an old Spanish toast.

"Amor, salud, dinero, y tiempo para gustarle.
Love, health, money, and time to enjoy it."

Dianna Booher, author of *Executive Portfolio of Model Speeches* (Prentice Hall Trade, 1992) and *Communicate with Confidence* (McGraw-Hill Trade, 1994), offers this wedding toast:

> Marriage is a commitment to life. To the best
> two people can give to themselves and to each
> other. Marriage deepens and enriches every
> detail of living. Fun is more thrilling. Happiness
> is fuller. Compassion is stronger. Forgiveness is
> faster. Laughter is richer. Sharing is deeper.
> Marriage has more potential than any other
> relationship for bringing out the best in
> ourselves and living life to its fullest. May your
> marriage bind you closer than any other
> relationship on earth.
>
> *(Toast #133 from* Executive Portfolio of
> Model Speeches.*)*

"Express your affection and good wishes for the individual. Focus on the other person, rather than yourself. Be brief."

Dave Broadfoot, award winning speaker, writer, and comedian is founder and veteran of the C.B.C. comedy, *Air Farce*; and star of the hit TV special, *Dave Broadfoot: Old Enough to Say What I Want*. He's provided two toasts he loves to use:

> What's beautiful may not always be good, but
> what's good is always beautiful. Here's to what
> we are about to eat—it's really good!

Nature gives us food,
magic transforms it into exquisite cuisine. Here's
to the magician!

"Give your toast while you're still sober—coherence helps."

Doc Blakely is the author of Doc Blakely's *Handbook of Wit and Pungent Humor* (Rich Publishing Company, 1983), *Push-Button Wit* (Rich Publishing Company, 1991), *Keep 'Em Laughin'*, and others.

Here's to the desert
And the valleys so green;
Here's to the cowgirls
And the cowboys so lean;
Here's to the ones we love
Dearest and most;
And God bless Texas—
That's a Texan's toast.

"Never toast a man who is holding a gun, never toast a woman with fangs, and never toast any person who drinks from a sack."

Willie Jolley, author of the national best-seller, *It Only Takes a Minute to Change Your Life* (St. Martin's Press, 1997), and host of the syndicated radio and television show, *The Magnificent Motivational Minute!*

My friend I wish health to you,
I also wish wealth to you;
I wish the best that life can give to you,
And may dreams always come true to you.
May fortune be kind to you,
And happiness be true to you;
And love be so sweet to you
And life be long and good to you.
And in this toast we give to you
Our love we all give to you.

"Make it brief, keep it short and sweet, make it simple and make it heartfelt."

Dr. Gayle Carson is the author of *How to Get to the Top and Stay There* (Lane Publishing, 1988).

My motto has always been:
"Be the best you can be,"
...whatever that is.

"Don't do anything so personal that it will embarrass the person involved, and always speak distinctly and loudly when you are giving the toast. (I have seen too many people mumble their way through [a toast], and no one can understand them.) Also, sometimes a private joke is too private, and no one gets it!"

Marjorie Brody is a professional speaker and seminar leader, and author of eight books, including *Speaking is an Audience-Centered Sport* (Career Skills Press, 2001) and *Complete Business Etiquette Handbook* (Prentice Hall, 1994). She says:

"My favorite toasts have been ones I have given for good female friends at their *second* marriages. Each has been spontaneous (hence no script here). Included have been stories of their relationships, the fact that some people just don't get it right the first time, husband number two has to try harder, etc. Although the toast is initially humorous, I end stressing the significance and joy of the occasion, and wish them well.

"If you want a polished presentation, prepare and practice the toast. Focus on three to five key points, then give examples. Although humor is effective, avoid jokes. Be careful you don't humiliate the receiver—slight embarrassment is okay, but say nothing they don't want the group to know about. Don't go on too long. Don't tell inside stories that the audience doesn't understand. It's fine to make them hit the heart, and be emotional, but end in an upbeat spirit."

Jack Canfield, coauthor of the *Chicken Soup for the Soul* series (Health Communications), offers this contribution:

> May you always work like you don't need the
> money; may you always love like you've never
> been hurt; and may you always dance like
> there's nobody watching.

"Speak from your heart, and don't be afraid to be spontaneous."

Steve Chandler, author of *100 Ways to Motivate Yourself* (Career Press, 2001), suggests this familiar but nearly universally applicable toast:

> God grant me the serenity to accept the things I
> cannot change,
> The courage to change the things I can change,
> And the wisdom to know the difference.

"Make sure you have a minimum of six drinks before delivering your toast, so you're not too shy to make it moving and dramatic."

Shep Hyken, professional speaker and author, suggests this toast for a wedding:

> Live each day as if it's your last, and each night
> as if it was your first.

"Be sincere and appropriate."

John Patrick Dolan, attorney-at-law, professional speaker, NSA member, offers:

> Here's to you and here's to me,
> And if we ever disagree,
> The heck with you! Here's to me!

"Get to the point—short and sweet toasts are preferable to boring, long-winded diatribes."

John Crudele, international presenter, author, and youth expert, reflects on drinking and toasting:

"One-third of all adults in America over the age of 26 consume zero alcohol. I, too, host an alcohol-free lifestyle, which I find affects the drink but not the toast.

"The tradition whereby someone is honored can be celebrated with everything from chilled milk or frothed cappuccino, to sparkling champagne substitute or frosty nonalcoholic beer. It's not the value of the drink that makes the memory, but rather the true feelings of sincere goodness in one's heart for another. Within the shared intimacies of the relationship, words of encouragement are likened to a prayer, as special meaning connects thoughts to hearts, and moments to lifetimes. Even the most mundane or trite becomes a celebration as friends bond, invoking good will for one's future. A simple, spontaneous gesture and thoughtful reflection now lingers in the mind as time stands still in the busyness of our worlds.

"Next time, when the moment arises for the lifting of a glass, let not the alcohol distract from the spirit of your toast, nor the lack of alcohol hinder the opportunity for souls to touch as tender memories are forever nurtured, shared, and savored."

W. Mitchell, author, television host, and speaker, reveals a toast that John Wilson, a friend and former Navy SEAL, shared with him:

> There are silver ships, there are gold ships,
> But there are no ships like friendships.

Cher Holton, Ph.D., certified speaking professional, management consultant, and self-described impact consultant, says:

> Here's to a recognition that it doesn't matter
> what great things you accomplish until you
> have inner peace; and once you have inner
> peace, it doesn't matter what great things you
> accomplish! May you have that inner peace
> throughout your life.

"Be enthusiastic, be sincere, and be short (in length, not height)!"

Art Fettig, motivational humorist and author of *How to Hold an Audience in the Hollow of Your Hand* (Growth Unlimited, 1984), offers three toasts:

To the volunteer

> Give a cheer, give a cheer, for the Volunteer,
> For while others say they'll see to it.
> Give a cheer, give a cheer, for the Volunteer,
> For they simply go out and do it.
> Give a cheer, give a cheer, for the Volunteer,
> They are brave, and they're ready for scrappin'.
> Give a cheer, give a cheer, for the Volunteer,
> They're the people who make things happen.
> Give a cheer, give a cheer, for the Volunteer,
> I think God sends them down from above.
> Give a cheer, give a cheer, for the Volunteer,
> Yes, they fill this whole world with love.

A toast to seniors

Here's to the Seniors,
Survivors all.
Many answered
The nation's call

In the World War,
Korea too,
When fighting was
The thing to do.

You danced to Goodman
And T.D.
You made America
Strong and free.

You raised your kids
The best you could.
In fact, you did
A world of good.

You worked, you sweat,
You did your share.
And now you wonder,
"Who's to care?"

Yes, here's to Seniors:
Let's give a cheer!
You get more loving
Year by year.

May the road come up to meet you,
May the wind be always at your back,
And may the wind at your back
never be your own,
Nor anyone else's.

Richard Hadden, coauthor of *Contented Cows Give Better Milk: The Plain Truth about Employee Reactions and Your Bottom Line* (Saltillo Press, 2000), notes,

"I am of Scottish ancestry, and my wife is a native Scot. The Scots probably invented the toast, and there are many Scottish and Gaelic toasts that we like. This first one is my personal favorite. It's called, 'There's Nae Luck Aboot the Hoose.'"

> May the best ye've ever seen
> Be the worst ye'll ever see.
> May a moose ne'er leave your girnal
> Wi' a tear drap in his ee.
> May ye aye keep hale and hearty
> Till ye're auld enough tae dee,
> May ye aye be just as happy
> As I wish ye aye tae be.
> *(Moose = mouse; girnal = pantry)*

"This is a popular Scottish toast that exudes the national pride of the Scots. It means something along the lines of, 'Here's to us; who else in the world is like the Scots? Not very many, and they're all dead anyway. What a shame!'"

> Here's to us!
> Who's like us?
> Damn few, and they're all dead.
> More's the pity!

> Lang may your lum reek...
> W' other folks coal.
> *(Lum = chimney, reek = smoke)*

"The following toast, called "The Toast Master's Companion," was first uttered in Stirling, Scotland, in 1822. It gives some insight into what was important in that day and place. It works as well in the United States as it does in Scotland."

May opinion never float on the waves
of ignorance.
May we look forward with pleasure, and
backwards without remorse.
May we never crack a joke to break a
reputation.
May we never suffer for principles we
do not hold.
May we live to learn, and learn to live well.
May we live in pleasure and die out of debt.
A head to earn and a heart to spend,
Health of body, peace of mind, a clean shirt,
and a guinea*.

*(*A guinea was one pound, one shilling—a little less than $2.)*

I drink to the health of another,
And the drink I drink to is he,
In the hope that he drinks to another,
And the other, he drinks to is me.

"Make the toast while you're sober; know the toast by heart well enough to speak it perfectly even if you're not sober; and if you make up your own toast, keep it short."

Keith Harrell, President and CEO of Harrell Performance Systems, and author of *Attitude is Everything: 10 Life-Changing Steps* (Harper Business, 2002), remembers his favorite toast given at a friend's wedding.

"The best man stood up and asked everyone else to stand. He then sat down and raised his glass in the air saying:

> I am sitting down because I wanted to look up to
> the happiness, to the love, and to the joy this
> moment brings us all. We toast to wonderful
> people, wonderful friends, and I pray that the
> joy we all feel at the present moment will
> outlast us all.

"If you're not naturally funny, don't try to be. Be sincere."

Doug Jones is an international speaker and seminar leader on sales and sales management.

> Hope for the best,
> Expect the worst;
> Life is a play,
> And we're unrehearsed!

"Remember for whom you toast: Direct your comments to that person primarily, while acknowledging the others secondarily...and deliver *slowly*!"

Danielle Kennedy, author of *Seven-Figure Selling* (Berkeley, 1996), comments:

"Being a good Irish girl, this is a favorite of mine. It makes me and everyone else feel special and loved.

Old Irish Blessing

May the road rise up to meet you,
May the wind be always at your back,
May the sun shine warm upon your face,
And until we meet again,
May God hold you in the hollow of his hand.

"Don't get sloppy. If you feel so inclined, have your understudy do the honors."

Dennis McQuistion, author, speaker, and PBS talk-show host, contributes a toast that he says is used mostly for birthdays, and has just the slightest sexual innuendo, which makes it somewhat titillating when guests are slightly inebriated, or about to be:

May you live as long as you want to,
And want to as long as you live.

"Be enthusiastic. Be unique and personal (unlike the above)."

Brian Lee, professional speaker and author of *The Wedding M.C.* (Custom Learning Systems, 1998), offers this outline for a perfect toast to the bride:

1. Introduce your toast. "Mr./Madame Master of Ceremonies, Head Table Guests, Ladies and Gentlemen, and especially (Bride's first name)."

2. Explain relationship between you and the bride.

3. Share two or three personal humorous anecdotes involving the bride growing up, dating, working, etc. (Don't overly embarrass.)

4. Point out a few of the bride's achievements, better qualities. Flatter her.

5. Perhaps offer a few words of advice to the groom on how to get along with the bride.

6. Wish her and the groom success and happiness.

7. Add any other appropriate comments.

8. Properly lead guests through the toasting:

   Ladies and Gentlemen, would you please stand (pause until they do) and raise your glasses to the bride.

"Above all, be certain to say, 'Ladies and Gentlemen, please raise your glasses in a toast to (person's name).' Audience will follow your lead as you sip from your glass."

Art Linkletter is the author of 26 books, and star of two of the longest running shows in TV/radio history, *People are Funny* (19 years) and *House Party* (26 years). He comments:

"My favorite toasts have changed through my career. Looking back, I now note that my toasts as a young man seemed 'smart-alecky' (and occasionally naughty). As a middle-aged man, they were more inspirational, and now as a senior citizen, my taste is toward the sentimental. A toast I use often, at gatherings of people over the age of 50, concerns friendship, because in our later years I find that family and friends are the greatest source of happiness.

Here's to Friendship

Make new friends, but keep the old;
Those are silver, these are gold.
New-made friends, like new wine,
Age will mellow and refine.
Brow may furrow, hair turn gray,
But friendship never knows decay;
For 'mid old friends, tried and true,
We once again our youth renew.
So cherish friendship in your breast;
New is good, but old is best.
Make new friends, but keep the old;
Those are silver, these are gold.

"Think carefully about where you will be giving your toast, and to whom. Some toasts can be roasts, providing there's no cruelty to the humor. There's no reason ever to hurt anyone, or offend them by the material you have selected."

Florence Littauer, award winning speaker and author of 25 books, including *Personality Plus* and *Silver Boxes: The Gift of Encouragement* (Word Publishing, 1989), says:

"My favorite toasts are ones that are uplifting, light-hearted, positive, and have a rhyme. Here is a sample toast that I gave to my friend Bill Peterson at the CBA Baker-Revell Dinner:

A Vessel for Noble Purposes

There are vessels for noble purposes,
Some for common use each day.
Some are of gold or silver,
Some are of wood or clay.
Some are fashioned from the mud,
Some pulled up from the mire.
Some have been perfected
Through the refiner's fire.

Bill has lived in such a way
That we can hear his potter say,
"I am so pleased with this lump of clay
Who's become perfected along the way,
Who's done so much for CBA."
So for Baker Books, and all of us here today,
We thank you, Bill, for coming our way.

"Be positive, lighthearted, complimentary, and encouraging. Use the words to build the person up. Use humor that is in good taste (not slanderous, sexual, or discriminatory). Avoid sarcasm, because that usually emphasizes the person's faults and humiliates him or her. Evaluate what will be said and make sure it will not hurt the person's feelings or be a disparaging remark."

Dr. Terry Paulson, psychologist, provides practical and entertaining programs on managing oneself and leading others through change. He frequently uses the traditional Irish blessing (variations are included on pages 28 and 32.) Here, he shows two other favorites:

A wedding toast for my son and daughter-in-law

One and all, lift your glasses.
Here is to the bride and groom:
To your long health, to shared laughter,
To the magical and meaningful memories
You will create together.
To the wings of love
That will let you soar even higher together
Through the peaks and valleys life provides.
Here is to the twinkle of love in your eyes
That reminds each of us of our love renewed.
May God bless you and keep you.
God-willing, may you live as long as you want to
And want to as long as you live.
And for this one day,
may your worn out smile muscles
Not cramp your lips so much
you can't kiss tonight.
With this toast,
as a community of friends and family,
We pledge our ongoing support and prayers.

Short wedding toast

To you both:
May the most you hope for
Be the least you receive.
May you live all the days of your life together.

Chuck Reaves, professional moderator, and frequent master of ceremonies for clients all over the world, offers some sound toasting advice:

"First of all, focus on the person being toasted. This is not about you, this is about them. If you do this, you will find your-self less nervous (because you will realize that the attention is on the recipient and not you) and you will be more sincere. Instead of making a presentation, you will be making a personal statement or tribute.

"Next, be yourself. What has worked for others may not work for you. If you are a naturally funny person, use humor. If humor does not come easily to you, it probably won't work well in a toast. When the humor fails, the attention is on the person making the toast, not the one being toasted. Use your vocabu-lary, your accent, and your natural style to make the toast. In all likelihood, your toast will not be on the evening news, so don't worry about being 'professional.'

"Finally, ask yourself, 'If this toast were given for me, how would I feel?' If you would feel warm, humbled, honored, etc., it is probably a good toast. If you would be embarrassed, intimi-dated, or thinking, 'Gee, I wish my parents weren't here...,' then it's probably not a good one."

Tim Richardson, presenter of outdoor learning and mind-stretching seminars for Personal and Professional Growth, recalls,

"My most memorable toast started with, 'I'd like to protose a post....' I was 17 years old and very nervous. My advice...Practice!"

David Rich, nationally recognized speaker, leading expert on persuasion and rapport, and author of *The Question to Everyone's answer, How to Stay Motivated on a Daily Basis!* (Kendall/Hunt, 1994) says, "My favorite toast is from the Old Testament of the Bible:

> May the Lord bless you and keep you;
> May the Lord make his face shine upon you
> and be gracious to you;
> May the Lord lift up his countenance upon you
> and give you peace.

"My advise to toasters is to be authentic. Be yourself. A toast can get so vanilla it loses meaning. A toast should reflect the genuine thoughts of the toaster."

Mary Beth Roach, professional speaker, who expertly inpersonates Mae West in many of her speeches:

> Here's to the kind of room I like—wall to wall men!
> —Mae West, when admitted to the
> exclusively male Friar's Club in Hollywood

"Check with the people you are toasting beforehand to see if there is anything they would *not* like you to say—this way you're sure to avoid tense, embarrassing situations. Also, make sure you are on target for the appropriateness of the toast for the occasion."

Lee Robert, coauthor of *Gendersell: How to Sell the Oppostire Sex* (Touchstone Books, 2000) and *Cavett Robert: Leaving a Lasting Legacy*, offers this:

Cavett Robert Toast

May the hinges of friendship never rust,
May the wings of love never tear loose a
feather,
And may this sacred circle of love
Grow deeper and stronger every year,
And not be broken as long as we live.
'Cause they tell me that a bell is not a bell
Until we ring it,
A song is not a song until we sing it,
Love was not put in our hearts to stay,
Love is only love when we give it away.
So here's to those we love,
And here's to those who love us,
And here's to those that we love
Who love those who love us.
So lets keep this circle of friends
And never forget
That life is our greatest gift,
And living nobly, our finest art.
And what we can do, we ought'a do,
And what we ought'a do, we can do;
And what we can do, and ought'a do,

I know we will do.

Good luck, God bless, I love every one of you.

>—Cavett Robert, Founder, National
> Speakers Association (Given with permission
> by Lee E. Robert, from *Cavett Robert:
> Leaving a Lasting Legacy*, 1998).

Dick Semaan, "Stand-up Speaker and Pop-up Toaster," is recipient of NSA's Council of Peer Award of Excellence and presenter of "You're Not getting Older, You're Getting Better," sponsored by Life Care Centers of America. He shares this toast:

> Here's to (person's name)... I wish you the best
> that life has to offer, the simple pleasures which
> can only be described in the one-syllable words:
> Love, Joy, Peace, Hope, Faith, Strength,
> Health, Zeal, and Life!
> May you experience the fullness of every day
> with passion, vision, and commitment. May you
> be better today than you were yesterday, but
> not as good as you'll be tomorrow.

"Always say and do the things that will focus the eyes and ears of the guests upon the one(s) being toasted. The toast is for the toastee, not the toaster."

Somers White, management consultant and professional speaker who has worked in 50 states and six continents, currently residing in Phoenix, contributes this short but compelling toast:

Here's to the "good old days"—which are now!

"We look back on those wonderful days of the past. Many times we do not stop to realize these are the good old days of later times, but we are experiencing them now."

Jeff Slutsky, author of *Streetfighting: Low-Cost Marketing* and *Out-Think, Don't Out-Spend the Competition*, recollects:

"At the reception, after a brief fanfare played, the announcer bellowed, 'Ladies and gentlemen, may I present for the first time, Mr. and Mrs. LeBoeuf!' Everyone stood up and applauded as Michael and Elke entered the room and took their seats at the head table. Next, [I] gave this toast:

> Perhaps one of the most exciting duties of the best man is to give the first toast. I know that Michael in particular was very excited when entering the room today because, in 20 years of professional speaking, this was his first standing ovation. You know, last night at the "awards banquet," Michael told us just how much he and Elke appreciated all of you being with them on this day. In fact, he said that your attendance

here was the best gift you could have given him. I
just wish he had told me that four weeks ago,
before I dropped 300 bucks on a piece of crystal.
But be that as it may, everyone now, please lift
your glass and join me in wishing Michael and
Elke a long and happy life together.

"A *toast* is a pledge of good intentions, a wish for good health
and good things to come to someone or some couple or group.
'Eloquence' is thought on fire," said the late Ken McFarland,
who is considered one of the premier speakers of the first half
of the 20th century. We have to have eloquence in our toasts,
and they must have a touch of class about them. A toast should
seize the moment. It should offer the audience a hallmark for
the occasion, something to take away and remember. It can come
as a clever story about the person or some humor that makes a
point.

"**Keep it clean.** Off-color material is inappropriate for this
type of occasion. After all, you are there to elevate the subjects to a higher level. Why pull the occasion down with poor
taste?

"**Beware of alcohol.** The very nature of many occasions in-
troduces alcohol as part of the festivities. If you are speaking,
avoid the booze. It thickens the tongue and will cause you and
your subjects embarrassment. Most of us have a tough enough
time speaking when we are stone sober. To throw booze into
the mix makes the occasion impossible.

"**Suit the toast to the occasion.** These are usually happy
events. The exceptions are those retirement parties where someone has been forced out of a company. Be sensitive to these
second-tier issues so that the event does not become a bashing
of the company or the subject of the roast.

"**Master's tips for a good toast or roast:** Below are some helpful hints in preparing for your toast or roast:

1. Know the time restraints going in, and suit your comments to the time provided.

2. Try to personalize your comments.

3. Quotes are excellent tools to make your points.

4. There is always room for humor at these occasions, as long as it is appropriate and relative.

5. Humility is the order of the day. After all, the toast is a pledge of good intentions and best wishes for those being toasted.

6. Sincerity is the most important singular attribute of your toast. Believe in what you are sharing."

—From *The Toastmasters International Guide to Successful Speaking,* by Jeff Slutsky and Michael Aun (Dearborn, 1997)

Jim Tunney, Ed.D., is "The Dean of NFL Referees," former president of NSA, and author of *Impartial Judgment* (Griffen Pub, 1995). He observes:

"Because of my association with pro sports, I am frequently called upon to 'say a few words' before a contest or challenge—either sports competitions, or missions launched by a corporation, organization, or community group. It is gratifying how often the following poem (by the world's most prolific writer, Anonymous) strikes the right chord. The toast, also a prayer, compels our energy toward honor and dignity—always a good direction to take.

Prayer of a Sportsman

Dear Lord,
In the battle that goes on through life,
I ask only for a field that is fair,
A chance that is equal to all the strife,
The courage to strive and to dare.
If I should win, let it be by the code,
With my faith and my honor held high;
But if I should lose,
Let me stand by the road,
And cheer as the winners go by.

"The number-one, never-to-be-ignored rule is to *fit the toast to the event*. Be alert to people's sensitivities. Familiarity, gender, age, religion, politics, and all such contextual elements deserve respect. The toast-giver who dares not respect catching an egg in his or her face. Remember as well, *a toast is a tribute, not a roast*, and a *short* tribute at that. It is not a eulogy, homily, or speech."

Al Walker, "A Big Man with a Big Message," past NSA president, humorous motivational, and inspirational keynote speaker:

"All of my toasts fall into one of two categories: They're either real rough and should only be used at bachelor parties—after everyone is solidly inebriated—or they are words from my heart that express the way I feel at that specific moment.

"Don't be silly; you can be funny, and probably should, but there's a difference between silly and funny. Silly usually either draws attention to you or puts down one of the honorees. Funny is usually self-deprecating or pokes positive fun at the honorees."

Mikki Williams is an internationally recognized speaker, consultant, author, trainer, entrepreneur extraordinaire, and mensch. Known for her flamboyant style and infectious energy, she is an inspirational humorist and business motivator.

"My theory is that speaker resources are everywhere, including bathroom stalls in Germany, when I was there delivering speeches. I have learned over the years to keep my eyes and ears open. Because I do a lot of consulting with speakers of all levels, I find most people to be very traditional in terms of research and resources. Being known as the consummate rule-breaker, heretic, nonconformist (you get the picture), I am thrilled to find little pearls of wisdom in as many out-of-the-way places as the unexpected allow. As a result, I am always aware of my surroundings, and have found as many 'jewels' in unconventional locales as my peers have found rummaging through library books and online reports. Often imitated, but never duplicated.

"In my opinion, toasts can easily be corny or overly sappy, and laughter is always the great equalizer and human bonding agent. That would be my advice to the toasters and toastettes."

Dave Yoho, CEO of Dave Yoho Associates, dean of modern sales training and motivation, and author of *How to Have a Good Year Every Year!* (Berkeley Press, 1991), shares the following toast he uses for individuals he knows well:

> You are a unique and precious being created by
> God for very special purposes. You are ever
> doing the best you can. You are ever growing in
> love and awareness. This day is yours. No one
> can take it away from you.

Here's another favorite:

> Peace is not a season.
> It is a way of life.
> May it be yours.
> If you search for the person.
> You would like to be,
> You may never get to enjoy the person you are.
> Peace.
>
> —From *How to Have a Good Year Every Year*

Chapter
2

Romantic Toasts
and Proposals

It is a well-known fact that most women possess an extra gene particularly devoted to romance. If you give a woman candlelight, fine wine, and a sumptuous meal, or even a mug of beer and a basket of wings, she will very likely be able to express her romantic and loving feelings in a spontaneous toast.

Men on the other hand seem to lack this specific gene, but contrary to what they might say, are well aware how much mileage can be gotten from a few well-chosen words. So, although this section has good ideas for women, it is really intended to help out the guys who may find themselves in situations where a toast is what is needed.

Romantic toasts should be delivered from the heart with a great deal of eye contact. If the truth be known, when two hearts are open to one another, whatever is said will be perfect. However, these toasts may help you in those moments when you want to be sure to be prepared.

Romantic toasts are good any time. If you want to celebrate something, or want to show your spouse, date, or lover some needed attention, or find that you have forgotten something significant, such as the third-month anniversary of the time that you first met, try some of the toasts in this chapter.

> To the one I love: May our lives together be
> blessed with happiness and peace.

> To us.

To your beautiful eyes: They are windows to a
beautiful soul.

May our love be as strong as the willow, and as
willing to bend.

If you are ever afraid, or feeling alone,
remember this night and how much I love you.

I have never wanted to be so close to another
human being that I would care more about
them than I do about myself. May we hold this
moment forever. To us.

To a wonderful man/woman, who is both a
friend and a lover.

Your eyes are like a country sky in the autumn.
When I am with you I feel free to be myself.
Here's to my best friend and only love.

To the woman/man who shares the good times
and bad. Here's to the good times.

When God created souls and sent them into the
world, he knew, all along, that someday our souls
would find each other.
To my eternal soulmate.

You have given me a home in your arms. Since
I met you, I have learned what it is to be loved.
God bless our lives together.

To our success. Without you, it would be
meaningless.

To our life together. As we walk the path of
life, always know my hand is within your reach.

May we always remember the blessings of love.

You are my rose and my candlelight. Wherever
you are there is love.

Here's to a fine meal,
A beautiful table,
Children asleep
And a movie on cable.

To the most beautiful person in the world.
Thank you for sharing my life.

The sun sets and rises in your eyes. To you.

You have been so supportive of my search for
myself. What I have discovered along the way is
that I love you. To you—and now—to us.

To you: My inspiration, my light, my love.

May you never know the pain of uncertainty.
You can always count on my love.

To all the memories we have shared and the
new ones we are creating.

With you I believe I can do anything. To us and
a life full of prosperity.

There are so many things I wish I could say to
describe how I feel about you. Please trust that
in these simple words are a lifetime of dreams.
To us.

You do the dishes, I'll tend to mine,
Here's to a partnership so divine.

To you. When I am with you the sky is more
blue, the grass is more green, and I feel the
overwhelming urge to smile.

You don't really know what you are missing
until you find what you have been waiting for.
To my dream.

Proposals

Women often propose marriage to their lovers but tradition
still has it that the man asks his love for her hand in marriage.
Whether they admit it or not, most woman like the idea of being
surprised with a ring and being asked to spend their lives with
someone special. It is a big deal and a moment that is intended to
always be remembered.

There are so many creative and unusual ways to propose. It is
amazing how the most reserved man will find a way to let loose
with a public proposal. Men have rented out billboards, hired
mariachi bands, hidden rings in precarious places, and a number
of other ways intended for maximum surprise appeal. One theory
is that the big splash is supposed to take the place of the actual
face-to-face, dry throat, is-she-or-isn't-she-going-to-say-yes proposal. If it is on a billboard, it is likely the chosen one will want to
avoid the public humiliation of saying no. Whereas a private proposal can lead to a quiet rejection.

So here are some suggested proposals that have enough of the
romance factor that they are likely to have the intended results.

Remember that down on one knee is a good effect, but it is more important that there be love in the eyes. Tearing up is also good. Take your lover's hand in yours, give it a soft kiss, and before you show her the rock, choose from the following:

> Throughout my life I have always believed there was someone special for me. Someone who would make me feel complete and who would inspire me to be my best. You are the most precious person in the world to me and I would like to spend my life with you....(show her the ring) Will you marry me?

> My Grandmother always said that "every pot has its cover," but I didn't believe her. Now I know that it is possible to find a perfect fit. You are my soulmate....(show her the ring) Will you marry me?

> When I saw how beautiful you are, I was enchanted; When I grew to know how beautiful you are inside, I fell in love; There has never been, and never will be, anyone as special in my life as you and I want to make you as happy as you have made me: (show her the ring) Will you spend your life with me?

Grow old with me!
The best is yet to be,
The last of life
For which the first was made.

Seal me in your heart with permanent betrothal,
for love is strong as death...it flashes fire, the
very flame of Jehovah. Many waters cannot
quench the flame of love...neither can the floods
drown it.
(Song of Solomon chapter 8 verse 6)
(Show her the ring) I will love you forever and I
hope you will become my wife.
[Don't worry about including attributions.]

We have been through many good times
together. We have gotten to know one another
in many different ways. One of the things I love
about you is that I can show you who I really
am and you love me anyway. At least I hope
you do because I have something I would like
to ask you....(show her the ring)
Would you consent to spending the rest of your
life with me?

To the woman I love today, tomorrow, and
forever. With this ring I hope to seal our love.
Will you marry me?

Chapter
3

Toasts for Bachelor and
Bachelorette Parties

Bachelor Parties

When a man becomes engaged and it gets close to the time to take the plunge, it is important that his friends, and sometimes relatives, give him a good and hearty send off. Toasting at bachelor parties can violate rules of decency if you are all close friends. If the groom's highly conservative future father-in-law is in attendance, it is truly a wise idea to not give the details of the groom's past. It is simply not nice to give away secrets—real or fabricated—if it is going to totally embarrass the groom or get back to his bride.

On the other hand, there is an expectation of some guy stuff, which could be raunchy. We won't get too blue here and none of our toasts begin with, "There once was a girl from Nantucket..." If the groom is in his 20s it is fun to rib him about all the things he will be missing. If the groom is over 30 it is fun to remind him of his fun and how it is finally catching up with him.

Everything should be good-natured because grooms have been known to slip out the back door never to return. Strippers can be fun, but keep an eye on things they do not get too out of hand. The best man should watch out for the groom's best interests, which means staying reasonably sober and getting the groom home safely.

Here are some bachelor party ideas:

> A piece of cowboy advice:
> There are two theories to arguing with a
> woman. Neither one works.

Here's to good, old whiskey,
So amber and so clear:
'Tis not as sweet as a woman's lips,
But a damn sight more sincere.

Here's to my future mother-in-law, who insists
on calling me a son—but I never let her finish
the sentence.

Here's to King Solomon, ruler and sage,
The wisest of men in history's age.
He had wives by the thousands,
And thought it was fun.
Here's to hoping you'll know
How to handle just one.

Here's to the woman of my dreams, who looks
like a million bucks...and was just as hard to
earn.

Here's to you, here's to me,
In hopes we never disagree.
But if we do, the hell with you...here's to me!

With a past like ours, who needs a future?
Well, my friend, yours is waiting for you, you
lucky dog.

Here's to love, a love that will linger.
I gave her the ring...
and she gave me the finger.

Here's to the man who takes a wife: Let him
make no mistake. For it makes a lot of
difference whose wife you take.

May all your ups and downs be between the
sheets.

Here's to giving up the things you dare
And learning how to never swear.

May your new life be hot enough to help you
forget your old life.

Here's to keeping your bride as close as you
keep your wallet.

Here's to good whiskey, good wine, lifelong
friends, and more good times.

To a beautiful bride, a good job, and good
friends to keep you from blowing it all.

May the single all be married and all the married be happy. Love to one, friendship to many, and good will to all.

May we all have the unspeakable good fortune to win a true heart, and the merit to keep it.

Marriage: The gate through which the happy lover leaves his enchanted ground and returns from paradise to earth.

Marriage: May its lamp ever be supplied by the oil of truth and fidelity.

To our friends: May the present have no burdens for them and the future no terrors.

Unselfish friendship: May we ever be able to serve a friend, and noble enough to conceal it.

To the Lady we love and the Man we trust.

To woman: The bitter half of the man.

To the bride: She needs no eulogy; she speaks for herself.

To marriage: The happy estate that resembles a pair of shears; so joined that they cannot be separated; often moving in opposite directions, yet always punishing anyone who comes between them.

Bachelorette Parties

If you are a man, skip this section because women do not want you to know their secrets. Bachelorette parties can be just as raucous as bachelor parties. Girls just want to have fun, and lighthearted fun and laughter is the goal of the evening.

It is not uncommon for a male stripper to be engaged for entertainment and we know of one bachelorette party (it wasn't Deborah's, wink wink) where the sister of the bride-to-be hired a male stripper. The bride was locked her up in the bathroom with him and told to scream like she was in ecstasy. This was especially funny because the bride's grandmother was in attendance and had the biggest laugh of everyone.

The gifts given at bachelorette parties are typically sensuous such as bubble bath, kama sutra powder, or massage oils for the wedding night, or funny gifts such as panties that play "Here Comes the Bride."

When it comes to toasting, the toasts are often good-natured male-bashing initiating the bride into what awaits her. This is a time to have fun. Of course if the party is more formal and serious, if anyone attends, you will want to stick to the all-occasion toasts or basic well-wishing.

Lengthy toasts from the heart are appropriate if time allows, but avoid anything that will embarrass the guest of honor to the point that it makes her cry. Blushing is okay, humiliation is not.

To my friend: I have known you through thick
and thin; now that you are getting married let's
hope that thick does not mean your husband's
head.

Never forget your friends,
The ones who know you best;
We are very happy to see
The end to your marriage quest!

Men are from Mars
and women are from Venus;
Never forget
that men think with their penis.

May your life be long and sunny, and your
husband fat and funny.

I'll drink to the gentleman I think is most
entitled to it; for if anyone can drive me to drink,
he can certainly do it.

Here's to friendships that never go out of style.
May we kiss those we please, and please those we kiss.

Here's to husbands and sweethearts.
May they never meet!

Men are somewhat like sausage:
Very smooth upon the skin,
But you can never tell exactly
How much hog there is within.

To the men I've loved,
To the men I've kissed,
And my heartfelt apologies
To the men I've missed.

Women's faults are many,
Men have only two...
Everything they say,
And everything they do.

Here's to the men we love,
And here's to the men that love us.
But the men we love
Aren't the men who love us,
So screw the men and here's to us!

To man: The only animal that laughs, drinks
when he is not thirsty, and makes love at all
seasons of the year.

Here's to God's first thought: Man!
Here's to God's second thought: Woman!
Second thoughts are always better.

To firm friendship in marriage: May differences
of opinion only cement it.

To active marriage: May the hinges of marriage
never grow rusty.

To friendship: May its bark never founder on
the rocks of deception.

To the Lady we love and the Friend we trust.

To woman: The fairest work of a great author;
the edition is large, and no man should be
without a copy.

May we all have the unspeakable good fortune to
win a true heart, and the merit to keep it.

Chapter
4

Wedding Toasts

A wedding is a once-in-a-lifetime event, even if done several times in one's lifetime. Whether it is a first marriage or third, the bride and groom will always face their commitment with hope and a sense of promise. Weddings have many associated activities that are wonderful opportunities for toasting. In fact, between engagement parties, showers, bachelor and bachelorette parties, rehearsal dinners, and the wedding receptions, by the end of the nuptials, it is likely that everyone will be "toasted" out.

We have separated this section into the three main events during which a toast is expected. They are:

1. The engagement party.

2. The rehearsal dinner.

3. The wedding reception.

When toasting at these distinct gatherings, keep in mind what they represent. Each has a different purpose ultimately leading to the joining of two lives into the state of matrimony. Even if you are a cynic, it is best to put your personal opinions aside, and to recognize that this is a time to revel in romance, sentimentality, and (as our adolescents refer to it) cheesiness.

Some humor is welcome as long as it is not masking ill-intentioned sarcasm. The bride and groom deserve to be in their own little world of love and perfection before they settle into a life of dirty socks, bad habits, battles over toilet seats, movie choices, and miscommunications.

As you look for your perfect toast for the occasion, make sure to skim all of the toasts in this section. Most of them can be adapted for any or all three of the toast opportunity categories.

According to Winifred Gray in her book *You and Your Wedding* (Bantam Book, 1985), proper wedding toast etiquette is as follows:

1. The father of the bride proposes the first toast to his daughter and his future son-in-law at the engagement party.

2. The host or father of the groom proposes the first toast to the bride and groom at the rehearsal party.

3. The best man proposes the first toast to the bride and groom at the wedding reception.

4. If the bride and groom are seated when toasts are proposed to them, they remain seated, even when others stand. After guests have responded to the toast, the bride and groom drink their wine.

Engagement Parties

The engagement is a time of dreams and excitement for the couple. It is also a time when courtship is made public and families become acquainted. This can be joyous or it can spell disaster. Think of the movie *My Big Fat Greek Wedding* and you'll get the picture.

Engagement parties can be overwhelming. While the bride and groom are the center of attention, most everyone is checking out everyone else to decide if the interloper bride or groom, will be a welcomed addition to the clan. They are also evaluating each other for extended family potential.

At the engagement party, the father of the bride proposes the first toast to his daughter and future son-in-law, but everyone who chooses can add their sentiments. You want to give the father the spotlight for the longest time, so follow his lead. There are exceptions for the elder patriarchs or matriarchs of the family because no one wants to tell them to shorten their toast; they have earned whatever attention they are given.

If you are going to offer a toast at an engagement party, make sure you are not drunk. Don't use it as an opportunity to embarrass anyone or display your jealousy of someone else's happiness.

At one memorable engagement party when the families met for the first time, the sisters of the groom-to-be took the opportunity to get back at him for years of mutual torment. They shared stories of all the most embarrassing moments. Toasting and roasting are two very different things. If you are going to roast, you need to use humor that others can relate to. You want the object of the roast to be able to laugh with the barbs and not to want to hide in the bathroom. You also do not want to cause trouble between the couple by indicating there may be confessions afoot.

A toast can be amusing or teasing if good-natured. Often a vignette or anecdote can be used to lead into a toast. During one of the Herman family engagement toasts, Deborah's grandmother began with some family folklore of the time that Deborah, as a toddler, and her close-in-age big brother, Larry, were playing with a large box. Deborah climbed into the box and it tipped upright with her in it. She said, "Larry, helpa me, helpa me!"

Larry calmly replied; "Do the best you can." This vignette led into a sweet toast about how to make a marriage work.

When you give an engagement toast or any toast before the knot has been tied, keep it short or prepare ahead of time. This is for everyone's protection. When you are sizing someone up to become a part of the family, your brain may be lagging behind your mouth. Do not use this time to comment on your philosophy of marriage, particularly if you have been divorced, and do not give advice except of a most general nature.

This is the time to make a good first impression so you can help your child, sibling, or friend navigate the waters of setting up house.

If you are the father of the bride-to-be and therefore the first to make a toast, you can use this time to be sentimental. Having your daughter marry is a huge event in your life. If you have been unable to express your feelings, now is the time. These ideas can certainly be adapted for toasts during the rehearsal dinner or at the wedding reception. However, you are the first in the spotlight here, so you may want to capitalize on this attention. Here are some ideas:

To my daughter:

> I remember when you were just a little girl and I felt as if I had to protect you from the world. As I see you with _____, I know in my heart that you will be safe and loved.

To my future son-in-law:

> Although it is difficult for a father to accept that his daughter is grown, I know that you will provide for her and share a loving home.

To my daughter:

> My daughter's engaged,
> Oh what a thrill.
> When the wedding is over
> I know who pays the bill.

To my future son-in-law:

> If my daughter loves you that is good enough for me...but I still want to wait for the full CIA report. Just kidding. I will settle for the FBI.

Formal engagement parties will allow for more toasting, but even the smallest gathering can be a chance for friends, siblings, mothers, grandmothers, aunts, and cousins twice removed, to express their thoughts and well wishes. Some of the nicest toasts can be in the form of poems. Even if they are hokey, or you are unable to rhyme. If they come from your heart, they will be appreciated.

My daughter:

> You were always rough and tumble,
> Playing in the dirt;
> You would always call for Daddy
> When your knee was hurt;
> Now you're planning marriage
> To your chosen beau;
> But there are certain things
> That I think he ought to know!
>
> Be good to my little girl,
> Be there through the tears;
> Marriage has its ups and downs
> So love her through the years;
> Share each other's triumphs,
> Share each other's woes;
> May you live with love and comfort
> And as the saying goes:
>
> May you both live as long as you want and
> never want for as long as you live.
>
> *(You can certainly add your own favorite saying or prayer here.)*

Other general toasts include the following:

> A toast to love, laughter,
> And happily ever after.

> May your joys be as bright as morning, and your
> sorrows but shadows that fade in the sunlight of
> love.

> Down the hatch to a striking match!

The mother and father of the groom are certainly welcome to toast the future bride and groom as are other family members and friends. If there doesn't seem to be enough time, there will be plenty of opportunities to add your sentiments at the other wedding parties and festivities.

Rehearsal Dinner

The rehearsal dinner is held for intimate friends and family and out-of-town guests. It is usually paid for by the parents of the groom, so the toasting is typically begun by the host. Unless the groom's father is very in touch with his feminine side, it is not likely the toast will be quite so sentimental as one from father to daughter. However, this is a good opportunity for a father to show his pride that his son is taking this important step toward manhood.

In other words, it is better to be supportive of his son than to publicly proclaim how he never thought the good-for-nothing would settle down with anyone. The father of the groom should never mention how many girlfriends his son had before selecting a bride, no matter how envious he might be. He should also be delicate in how he refers to his son's future bride. There is a big difference between saying, "She is such a lovely young woman," and "He really got himself a hottie." Fathers and sons often have a secret language that may not be appropriate for this kind of gathering, and all attempts at humor should be well thought out.

The host for the evening should also begin his toast with recognition of those people who came in from out of town for the event. Weddings and other such events are sometimes the only time some family members are able to see each other.

Orchestrate your acknowledgments to make sure you do not forget anyone. It is amazing how people notice and do not forgive such slights. It is always a good idea to make guests feel special.

In toasting out-of-towners, you can try some of the following:

Over the miles we are always warmed by your
caring and blessed by your company for such a
special occasion.

What would a family event be without you? You
are an important flame for our candle.

We are glad that you were able to join us at this
festive table.

The bride- and groom-to-be can toast and acknowledge their families at a rehearsal dinner. It is also equally important for the bride and groom to welcome out-of-town guests and special friends. Weddings are about the happy couple, but they are also about showing appreciation and giving thanks.

Rehearsal dinners can be a lot of fun because they are the beginning of the festivities that directly lead up to the ceremony. The bride and groom are jittery and everyone becomes caught up in the fun, the romance, and the optimism.

This is another time when you might want to steer clear of too many embarrassing childhood stories. Oh, what the heck. As long as you avoid stories of toilet training, this is probably a good time to bring a little humor into the party. Everyone is more upbeat and there is likely to be less nervous scrutiny present by this time. This is a rite of passage for the couple, and they deserve a little ribbing. If they can't take it, they should run off to the court-house. Once a couple agrees to a sizeable wedding involving relatives, they have to be prepared for anything.

Possible rehearsal dinner toasts of the sentimental kind:

> In everyone's life there are things that go for the worse, then comes a love that can make everything better. Now that you have committed to a lifetime of sharing for better or for worse, may you always see that together is for the better.

> May the bridge you build together span a lifetime.

> To the happy couple, may you remember the joy you feel today so you can hold it in your hearts.

> Tomorrow as you share your vows, may your hands and hearts be joined in love.

Your lives have led you to the perfect love; one
that gives you the trust to see a future that can
only be filled with each other.

On the lighter side:

Tonight may be your rehearsal but tomorrow is
the real deal.
Make sure you get it right because there are no
refunds or returns.

Here's to the couple: a lovely pair,
Both of them nervous to death.
Let us continue to drink to your life,
As you sneak out and catch your breath.

Remember: If you are going to use an anecdote as a lead-in to
a toast, make sure it is not mean-spirited or too much of an "in"
joke that no one else will understand or relate to. Make sure to
end it with some kind of well wishing for the couple.

The Wedding Reception

If you are asked to give a toast at a wedding reception, keep in
mind that most couples who have weddings of any significant
size typically preserve the memories of their special day on video.
If for no other reason, avoid drinking heavily before delivering
your wedding toast or you can be sure you will never live it down.
Wedding toasts can be humorous if you avoid being too personal.

If you are having a traditional wedding and want to follow the
typical order of toasts, it is as follows:

- ♈ The best man.

- ♈ The groom's father.

- ♈ The bride's father.

- ♈ The groom.

- ♈ The bride.

- ♈ The maid of honor.

- ♈ The groom's mother.

- ♈ The bride's mother.

As you can see, that is a lot of toasting. This is why you will want to keep your toasts short. Toasting typically does not start until after some kind of cocktail reception while the guests are waiting for the bride and groom and various family members to finish being congratulated through a traditional receiving line. There are also photo ops to consider. After the ceremony, the photographer will likely corner the bride and groom for formal photographs before anything ruins the pristine moment. Veils come off, trains are removed, and things can spill.

This can take a while. The point is that while the photographer is taking a shot of the bride and groom's hands to show off their rings, the guests are getting "toasted." By the time the actual toasting begins, it is easier to keep the audience's attention by not pontificating. The toast is intended to wish the couple well, not to show off your skills at oration.

On the other hand, you do have a captive audience. While you won't sustain undivided attention for long, it is your opportunity to express your feelings. As with any of the wedding-related events, it is natural and wonderful to be caught up in the moment.

The best man is expected to make the most important toast. At this time the parents take a back seat to the special relationships the bride and groom have as a couple and as individuals. It would be fine if, in the interest of equality, the bride and groom ask the maid of honor to follow this toast with one of her own.

The best man has the most leeway for length. We don't have to remind, but of course we will, any best man to avoid anything humiliating, overly sexual, or specifically insulting. A little humor and generic, good-natured insults are fine. Here are some examples of wedding toasts:

> May your hearts beat as one from this day
> forward.

> On a cold winter's day, two porcupines huddled
> together to stay warm. Feeling one another's
> quills, they moved apart. Every time the need
> for warmth brought them together, their quills
> would drive them apart. They were driven back
> and forth at the mercy of their discomforts,
> until they found the distance from each other
> that provided both a maximum of comfort and
> a minimum of pain.
> May your need for warmth be satisfied, and you
> be spared the stab of your lover's quills.

> Here's to the bride and groom, a case of love
> pure and simple: (Bride) is pure and (Groom)
> is simple.

> To (Groom), the luckiest man on earth, and to
> (Bride), the woman who made him that way.

> Here's to marriage, for man is not complete
> until he is married...and then he's finished!

To your wedding: May your love for each other grow as surely as your waistlines will.

You see each other now as the fulfillment of your dreams. May you have the understanding that today you begin your lives, and there are dreams you have yet to share.

As you build your home together may you use the best of what each of you bring to your union and may you accept everything that is left.

Here's to the bride and groom!
May you have a happy honeymoon,
May you lead a happy life,
May you have a bunch of money soon,
And live without all strife.

Marriage is a wonderful institution—but who wants to live in an institution?

May we all live to be present at their golden wedding anniversary.

May you grow old on one pillow.

Give what you can, take what you will,
When all's said and done,
You both pay the bill.
May you have a wonderful life together.

May your love be as endless as your wedding
rings.

May your wedding days be few, and your
anniversaries many.

May your arguments be as long-lived as my
New Year's resolutions.

To the Fate that brought you together, and the
Love that will keep you happy forever.

May the joy you feel today be a pale shadow of
that which is to come.

"Nothing is nobler or more admirable
Than when two people, who see eye to eye, live
together as husband and wife,
Thereby confounding their enemies and
delighting their friends."

—Homer, from *The Odyssey*

May your marriage be wrapped in angel's wings
and all good things.

Love is like a garden. It will continue to grow
wild but flourishes best with attention. May
your garden always remain in full bloom.

May your love be modern enough to survive the
times, and old-fashioned enough to last forever.

Here's the husband, here's the wife:
May they remain lovers for life.

Although outside it is cold and wintry, inside
(Bride) and (Groom's) hearts it is warm, and
today the seeds of love have been planted.
As the spring flowers are soon to bloom, may
your love flourish like a sunny season that
never ends.

May you be as one soul: arms around one
another and eyes toward heaven.

May you live together happy and free as the
rolling waves on the deep, blue sea.

From the groom or bride:

Today, from you and from me, we have made *us*.
What you now do, and what I now do, we do for
us. Although you are still you, and I am still me,
it is the union of *us* that is the guide along life's
journey and beyond. We do for *us*—our every
thought is for *us*—now and for always.

As two become one—love is eternal.

May you never lie, cheat, or drink.
But if you must lie, lie in each other's arms.
If you must cheat, cheat death.
And if you must drink, drink with all of us
because we love you.

The Divine brought you together for a blessed
reason. May your marriage create a permanent
dwelling place for love.

Marriage is a lot like the army: Everyone
complains, but you'd be surprised at the large
number that reenlist.

(Bride), please put your hand on the table. Now
(Groom), put your hand on top of (Bride's)
hand. I want everyone in the room to see the
last time that (Groom) has the upper hand!

May you share a joy that grows deeper, a
friendship that grows closer, and a marriage that
grows richer through the years.

May the road you now travel together be filled
with much love and success.

May you share equally in each other's love,
and may all your troubles be little ones.

May your hands be forever clasped in
friendship and your hearts forever joined
in love.

Let us live for the future
And learn from the past.
The knowledge you gain
Will make your marriage last.

Perchance to dream, perchance is right!
You won't get a chance to dream tonight.

May your love be everlasting, and your home
filled with patience, acceptance, and surpassed
expectations.

May your good times be plenty,
Your sad times be few;
May your love grow brighter with each day,
And with each day begin anew.

As you set out to write a new chapter in your
life as husband and wife, may your union be
like a game of poker: Start as a pair and end
with a full house.

I would like to thank the parents of the bride
and groom, for without them, this day would
not be possible.

On this your wedding day, we wish you a
one-way ticket on the love train.

Here's to the bride and mothers-in-law;
Here's to the groom and fathers-in-law;
Here's to the sisters and brothers-in-law;
Here's to the brothers and sisters-in-law;
Here's to good friends and friends-in-law;
May none of them need an attorney-at-law!

We wish them the best of luck,
But know that they don't need it,
Because they have the best of love.

May your love build for you an indestructible
community of two, and may your married life
be as loving as it is long. To the bride and
groom!

Roses are red, violets are fine, hope your
marriage is as happy as mine.

Let us toast the health of the bride,
Let us toast the health of the groom.
Let us toast the person that tied,
Let us toast every guest in the room.

"Look down you gods
And on this couple drop a blessed crown."
                    —William Shakespeare

A commitment should last forever, and life
should always be this good. But when times are
hard and the road is rough, remember the
words you spoke today, remember the way you
feel right now, and try to forgive. Sometimes
that's all we have to give. For to love is to learn,
and to learn is to forgive. Best wishes to you
both, and may your love be long-lived.

May all your children have wealthy parents!

I wish both of you the patience of Job,
The wisdom of Solomon,
And the children of Israel.

To the beautiful bride:
May she always stay happy and nice,
With all the love in her eyes,
Not to mention being so witty and wise;
Of that no one can deny,
Especially the groom, that's why.

And to the handsome groom:
May he stay as romantic and true;
A husband, the role he'll assume,
Tell him, for he has no clue;
Every day a flower or some perfume,
To make her smile and never be blue.

And here's to the groom with the bride so fair,
And here's to the bride with the groom so rare,
May every day be happier than the last!

Never above you, never below you,
Always beside you.

May you always be each other's best friends,
May your honeymoon be filled with smiles
and laughter,
And may you live happily married ever after.

Don't look for the perfect spouse in each other,
try to be the perfect spouse for each other.

May your marriage be like fine wine, getting
better and better with age.

Here's to (Bride and Groom):
May your years together be as wonderful
as today,
May your sorrows be few and your joys
be countless.
And may a flight of angels carry you as one
from this day forward.

May you both have the patience to listen.

May the sparkle in your eyes light your path for
the years to come.

To the groom:
The great philosopher Confucius once said,
"Bigamy means having one wife too many."
Some say monogamy means the same thing.

May your obstetrician find your babies so
beautiful that he delivers them free!

May you live long lives, doing what you love together. And when the time comes for you to pass away, may you die as you lived, doing what you love together.

I would wish you good luck, but I never wish luck on a sure thing.

Standing next to each other, facing the world, and you always able to say, "This is my beloved, this is my friend."

They say that marriage is an institution.
And I can't think of two people who should be institutionalized more than this bride and groom.

May the twinkle in your eyes stay with you, and the love in your hearts never fade.

...And remember, during any disagreement the husband is entitled to the last few words. And those words are, "Yes, dear."

May you always be lovers,
But most of all friends,
And share with each other whatever life sends.

As you make your way through life together,
hold fast to your dreams and each other's
hands.

To the happy couple: May your needs be few,
and your blessings be many.

May your lifetime together
Be full and complete,
And your kisses together
Be deep, warm, and sweet.

To the Bride and Groom:
May you have the *courage* to create a life
unique to your vision of the world;
May you have the *tolerance* to allow the other
to grow, according to his or her own path; and at
his or her own pace;
May you understand that *self protection* does
not mean mistrust;
May you each have enough *self love* to receive
the love each has to give;
May you grow beyond the limits of your
individual *egos* to fully surrender to love;
And may you both embrace the *God love* that
forms the center of your union.

—Excerpted from *Spritual Writing from
Inspiration to Publication* by Deborah
Herman (Beyond Words Publishing, 1998).

(Bride) and (Groom) are like epoxy: Separate
they are perpetually sticky, like sap. But together
they form a rock-hard bond.

May the love you share forever remain as
beautiful as the bride looks today.

A toast to our Bride and Groom:
Perfect, total love between a man and woman
is like a flaming ball of fire, composed of four
layers.
The outer layer of the ball of love is the flame
of passion for one another. May you possess it
all of your lives.
The second layer of the ball is that of liking
each other, with its ebbs and flows. May your
ebbs always be less frequent than your flows.
The third layer is that of friendship. May you
always find your best friend in each other.
The fourth and inner layer is the hard, firm
core of decision, shown to us perfectly by our
Lord. This is the same love found in the Bible, in
Corinthians 13. May you be constant in your
decision to love each other always. And may
you have this perfect, total love forever.

May the garden of your life together need very
little weeding.

To keep a marriage brimming,
With love in the loving cup,
Whenever you're wrong, admit it,
Whenever you're right, shut up!

Now you will feel no rain, for each of you will be
shelter to the other. Now you will feel no cold,
for each of you will be warmth to the other. Now
there is no more loneliness. Now there are two
persons, but one life before you. Go now to your
dwelling, to enter into the days of your life
together. And may your days be good and long
upon the Earth.

—From an Apache Indian Wedding
Ceremony

May your joys exceed your sorrows, may your
ecstasy exceed pain, may your unselfish love
exceed your selfishness, may you live for the
sake of each other, and may the bounty of this
life be in abundance!

May all your days be filled with sunshine, all
your nights with romance, and all the time in
between with love. The love of your parents
has brought you this far; now may your love
for each other carry you forward this day and
always.

Here's a toast to the lovely bride,
And to the husband by her side.
Here's a toast to the home they are going
to share,
May love and trust dwell with them there.
Here's to the husband, here's to the wife.
May they remain lovers all of their life.

Same-Sex Weddings and Commitment Ceremonies

When we asked one of our lesbian friends if there is a particular protocol to toasting at a same-sex wedding, she emphatically replied that a wedding is a wedding. However, as we talked further about it, we discovered some important things to consider.

First of all, same-sex marriage per se, as of the time of this edition, is not recognized in any of the 50 states. However, there are ways to form legal domestic partnerships, for example, some states recognize "civil unions" between same-sex couple, but a wedding is usually a commitment ceremony publicly proclaiming the choice to live together as a "married" couple even though not afforded the legal recognition and legal rights of heterosexual couples.

If you are attending a same-sex wedding and are not a close friend, you will likely not be asked to give a toast so you don't have to worry any more than you would at a heterosexual wedding. However if you are straight and a close friend or relative, it is best to steer clear of same-gender references unless you can include them without making a fool out of yourself.

So if you are toasting at a same-sex wedding it is obvious to everyone attending that the couple are of the same gender. So toast with any toast that is caring and focused on a happy life and future together.

Just remember that no matter what gender or sexual preference, a wedding is a joining of two people who love each other. So revel in that and enjoy the event to the fullest. A toast from the heart will always be welcomed.

Chapter
5

Anniversary
Toasts

If you are toasting a couple on their anniversary, the couple receiving the honor should be afforded the same joy and illusion of romantic possibilities no matter what the circumstances of the lives together might be. In other words, if you are throwing a 40th wedding anniversary party for your parents and, although you love them, you know they more closely resemble the WWE wrestlers than Ozzie and Harriet, it's neither the time nor the place to behave like your inner child. Anniversary toasts can be amusing but should never be insulting.

The best-loved anniversary toasts are those that bring the couple back to the time they said their I do's. If the couple is particularly romantic, you can adapt any of the wedding toasts to fit the occasion.

General Anniversary Toasts

Here's to you both,
A beautiful pair,
On the birthday of
Your love affair.

Let anniversaries come, and anniversaries go—
but may your happiness continue forever.

Here's a toast to the many good times you've enjoyed together...and to the one or two that you just tolerated.

May the warmth of your affections survive the
frosts of age.

To your future anniversaries—may they be
outnumbered by your future pleasures.

Here's to the man who loves his wife,
And loves his wife alone.
For many a man loves another man's wife,
When he ought to be loving his own.

Let us drink to love, which is nothing unless it is
divided by two.

Here's to the husband,
And here's to the wife:
May they be lovers for life.

Love doesn't make the world go around;
love is what makes the ride worthwhile.

A toast to your anniversary: You've had many
good years together, either that or one hell of a
prenuptial agreement.

The love you give away
Is the only love you keep.

May your love be as endless as your
wedding rings.

New love is silver,
Wait for the rest;
Old love is gold love,
Old love is best.

May the rest of your lives be like a bed of
roses...without the thorns.

A toast to your anniversary and the love that
has held you together these many years:
When times are good,
It's easy, brother.
When times are tough
Is when you need one another.

To marriage: an exercise that works every
muscle in the human spirit.

May you love each other more than yesterday,
but less than tomorrow.

May you always look into each other's eyes as you did the night you first met.

Joy to you on your anniversary. From this day forward may you be blessed with the same happiness your union has brought to those around you.

Love each other as you would your children: unconditionally!

May the twinkle in your eyes stay with you, and the love in your hearts never fade.

May you have the best life has to offer.

May you be blessed with happiness and love that deepens every year.

May you celebrate a very happy anniversary with tender moments, love, and cherished memories.

May your love be reflected in the souls of your children.

To a couple who has been an inspiration to all of us. You reflect how wonderful love and union can be.

The lights are low, the kids are grown.
May you have many nights to call your own.

Some anniversaries are silver, some anniversaries are gold, but the best anniversaries to hope for are the ones where you grow old. To the happy couple, may you have many more healthy and happy years together.

To our parents: You probably never thought you'd survive the noise, the tussles, and the extra stuff in your house. On your anniversary we want you to know that we are all planning to move back in.

To the wonderful couple who shows the rest of us what love is all about.

I have known the groom for a long time. He is a man of honor, humor, and integrity. Though honor and integrity make the man, my toast is to humor, which makes the marriage.

You see each other now as the fulfillment of
your dreams. May you have the understanding
that today you begin your lives, and there are
dreams you have yet to share.

To a wonderful couple. Thank you for inviting us
to share your day. Always remember the love
your friends and family feel for you and know
that we will be there to help you through the
rough spots. We will also be there to bask in the
joy of a life created from two separate paths.

Toasting Each Other on Your Anniversary

Anniversaries are an occasion where couples may choose to
be alone away from other people and especially away from children. No matter what life is like during the day, the anniversary
celebration is the time to focus on each other. However, this is a
time when the romantic expectations of the wife may exceed
the romantic inclinations of the husband. This is a very good
time for a husband to order some wine or champagne or whatever does it for you, and raise his glass to toast his bride as he
did when they first declared their love. The right toast at the right
time will set the tone for the evening and even the next year.

The following are some examples of short toasts that can certainly be interchangeable for the husband or wife, but husbands
should definitely memorize one or two.

As with marriage proposals, lengthier toasts indicating how
much your life together means to you and how you build your
life around your love are always recommended. Never forget
why the two of you are together. Life can certainly slip into apa-
thy, which is another word for acute boredom. An anniversary is
an opportunity to restore some fire.

When I look into your eyes I see the flame of my
own passion;
I will never forget the day you consented to be
my bride.
That one should definitely earn some husband
points.

To my beloved on our anniversary. I love you
more with every passing year.

As Einstein said, time is a relative thing.
When I was searching for you, my perfect mate,
it moved too slowly. But now that we are
together, it moves at the speed of light. To my
spouse on our anniversary.

Here's to loving, to romance, to us:
May we travel together through time.
We alone count as none, but together we're one.
For our partnership puts love to rhyme.

Here's to you who halves my sorrows and
doubles my joys.

To my beloved on our anniversary. I love you
more with every passing year.

To my twin soul. As the years pass, we become
more and more as one.

I thought I would forget who I was after our
marriage, but I realize I have become who I am
because of it. May our years together continue to
bring out the best in each other.

To the woman I would marry over and over
again.

Though I am not so sentimental
As we mark our wedding day,
I toast our life together
With the thoughts I may not say.

To my husband who gets so much better
every day that you would never imagine how
he started out before I came along.

Chapter
6

Birthday Toasts

No matter what our age, everyone loves to feel special on his or her birthday. The older we get, the more important it is to us to be recognized no matter how much we protest.

Birthdays are great opportunities for toasts of all kinds. When young people have significant birthdays such as age 16 or 21, it is perfectly acceptable to make them the subject of reasonable jokes or roasts. But keep in mind that if the birthday boy or girl is over 30, you may be stomping on sacred territory. Not everyone has a thick skin about certain aspects of aging. For example, toasts referring to anything sagging are to be reserved for only the closest of friends. Even then they can be risky.

Otherwise, birthday toasts leave a lot of room for creativity. As long as you show your appreciation for the fact that your friend or loved one was born, you have accomplished your goal. As with any toast, stories are great and spontaneity is welcome, but always think of tomorrow and what the ramifications are of any ill-chosen words. As you drink your way through the celebration, make sure your brain remains engaged before your mouth does the talking.

The best kind of toast is always one from the heart so feel free to be sentimental. You can always adapt any of the romantic toasts to suit the occasion.

Here are some birthday toasts to get you started.

> To wish you joy on your birthday
> And all the whole year through
> For all the best that life can hold,
> Is none too good for you.

Many happy returns
Of the day of your birth;
Many happy blessings
To brighten your pathway on earth;
Many friendships to cheer
And provoke you to mirth;
Many feastings and frolics
To add to your girth.

May you die in bed at 95 years old shot by a
jealous husband.

80th birthday or any birthday after 50:

My *(husband, wife, friend, grandmother…)*
is 80
And still doesn't need glasses,
She is happy to drink out of the bottle.

To you on your birthday:
You're not too old when your hair turns gray.
You're not too old when your teeth decay.
But you'll know you are ready
for that final sleep,
When your mind makes promises
your body can't keep.

May you live forever, may I never die.

"A man is only as old as the woman he feels."
                                        —Groucho Marx

You're not as young as you used to be,
But be glad you're not as old as you are going
to be.

To a healthy year, and many of them.

Health to you, wealth to you,
The best that life can give to you.
Happiness be true to you,
And life be long and good to you.

To a great age—old enough to know better,
young enough not to care.

To the birthday boy/girl. May all your days be
filled with wonderment.

May the only lift your face needs be provided
by your smile.

To _____: If life begins at 40, we can't wait
to see how you'll top what has come before.

May we all be together to toast your 100th year.

To silly thoughts and birthday rhymes,
Your special day and our good times.

To someone who deserves a special day: Go for
the gusto, put the must-dos away.

May your life be filled with friends, love,
and family.

The trick to getting older is to grab each
moment as if it were your last.
Sooner or later it will be.

Wrinkles on your forehead,
A roll around your middle,
A bright high-powered sports car,
Makes your true age noncommittal.
Happy birthday, you old goat.

May your birthday wishes come true and your
mother-in-law win a year-long cruise around
the world.

Emeralds, pearls, diamonds, and lace—you'd
trade them all for a younger face.

When the ocean tides change with the phases
of the moon, so are we reminded of the cycles
of our days.

On your birthday, do unto yourself as you
would have the world do unto you.

Birthdays are never like this when I have them.
Although another year has passed,
She's no older than the last!

May everything about your day be just the way
you want.
Have a happy and wonderful birthday and life.

Another candle on your cake?
Well, that's no cause to pout.
Be glad that you have strength enough
To blow the darn thing out!

With love to you on your day of days,
We lift our glasses to sing your praise.

There are some people who pass through your
life like a butterfly.
They rarely make contact
and then are quickly gone.
There are those who pass through your life like
fellow travelers.
They sit and talk for a while on the airplane,
but upon touchdown, they drift away toward
their own destinations.
Then there are people who pass through your
life and decide to set up camp.
They work with you, share with you, borrow
from you, care about you.
These are the kind that give meaning to life.
(Name) falls into that latter category.
To my dear friend, I wish a happy birthday and
an exciting rest of his/her life.

Here's to birthdays: They're not so bad,
considering the alternative.

Another year older? Think this way:
Just one day older than yesterday.

You're only as old as you are.

To your birthday, glass held high;
Glad it's you that's older, and not I.

Someone has said that a friend is someone who understands your past, believes in your future, and accepts you today just the way you are. (Name) has been just that kind of person. That's why his birthday is as special to me as my very own.

Happy birthday to a very special person.

Here's to you! No matter how old you are, you don't look it!

Birthdays are a time to celebrate the memories of days gone by, the joys of the moment, and the dreams of tomorrow. We're celebrating with you.

You are now a (man, woman). May you be blessed with the confidence that you can learn from your mistakes.

May you live to be 100 years old, with one extra year to repent.

Just remember that when you get over the hill, you pick up speed on the downside. But you have no cause to worry. The faster you go, the better you get. Here's to a great birthday.

There's a time to be born and a time to die, and what happens in between is of great importance. (Name), of all the people I know, you've made the most of that interval. Just think of this birthday as a green light on the road of your dreams. Happiness to you.

In many ways, (name), you've been like a son/daughter to me—pouty, arrogant, disrespectful. Seriously, I'd be awfully proud to have a son/daughter just like you. Here's to a happy, happy birthday.

To a (brother, sister): I am honored to call him/her my friend.

To a wonderful (brother, sister) who has always been good enough to be older than me.

From father to son, or from mother to daughter:

When you were born I saw in you all of the
things I had dreamed for myself.
Now I see that you are more than I could
have imagined.
Happy birthday (son, daughter).
May all of the dreams you have for yourself
come true.

A health to our dearest: May her purse always be heavy and her heart always light.

Though you see yourself as getting older, we see your birthday as a reminder of how many happy times you have brought into our lives.
To many more birthdays that we can share with you.

May you live to be 120.

Thank you (dad, mom) for always being there for me. On this, your special day, may you be wined and dined like royalty but remember to give the bill to my (brother, sister).

For a significant birthday representing a change in a person's status (for example, 10, 13, 16, 18, 21), you can say the following:

As you reach this new chapter in your life, may you discover that it is you who will write your own story and may you always have a pencil on hand.

To a friend who has taught me what it must be like to have a (brother, sister).

"May you live to be 100 and may the last voice
you hear be mine."

—Frank Sinatra

To a happy future: May the best day we have
seen be worse than the worst that is to come.

"Happy birthday, my love.
Happy birthday, little girl grown tall.
And a kiss for every candle on your cake.

"May your birthday wish come true,
May the fates be kind to you
And whatever I can do
you can count on.

"Happy birthday, my love,
You have friends that care about you
Who would hate to do without you, so you see
We love you through the laughter
And the tears that may come after,
And a special happy birthday, love,
from me."

—Steve Allen

Happy Birthday to you,
And many to be,
With friends that are true
As you are to me.

To enduring prudence: May the pleasures of
youth never bring us pain in old age.

Do not resist growing old; many are denied the
privilege.

Bris

In the Jewish tradition, when a baby boy is born, eight days
after the birth there is a ceremony called a bris (b'rit milah).
This is where the baby boy becomes a "child of the covenant."
The baby is ritually or actually circumcised, and there is a community or family celebration. This is a joyous occasion and, aside
from the kiddush (the blessing over the wine as part of the ritual),
it is a time when a family member or guest can say a few words
of congratulation. Mazel Tov (good luck) or L'Chaim (to life) are
both good, but here are some other suggestions:

Father of fathers, make me one,
A fit example for my son.

May you live to introduce your son to Torah, to
marriage, and to good deeds.

May your son always be as a blessing to you and
to the community.

Bar or Bat Mitzvah

Becoming a Bar or Bat Mitzvah are rites of passage when a Jewish boy or girl, upon reaching the age of 13, take his or her place as a member of the community. They essentially become a "child of the commandment." The ceremony, where the boy or girl lead the service and read from the Torah for the first time marks this occasion. Most families have a celebration following the service that ranges from modest to something similar to a wedding. This event is certainly an occasion worth a toast. The toast can refer to the parents or to the Bar or Bat Mitzvah child. The essence should be of pride for the accomplishment, of well wishing, and of welcoming. If you are not Jewish, do not worry; there is no particular protocol. It is a happy occasion, so fun is allowed. Here are some ideas:

To you a great big Mazel Tov,
A blessing and a cheer.
Your family all are kvelling,
At the joy that you've brought here.

As you now enter your new life as a
Son/daughter of the commandment,
May you be blessed with Torah, family,
and community.
With these things your life will always be full.

Today you are a man/woman.
You no longer have to sit at the kid's table.

Chapter
7

Toasts for Friends

Giving a toast on behalf of a friend can be fun and rewarding. It is so easy to take friendship for granted. When you have an occasion to raise a glass, bottle, or keg of something in good cheer to someone you care about, even the least touchy-feely among us can let fly with some sentiment.

Buddies and girlfriends are a very important part of life. Aside from gender-bashing toasts reserved for girls' and guys' nights out, there may be times when you want to say something meaningful.

> Here's a toast to the future,
> A sigh for the past;
> We can love and remember,
> And hope to the last.
> And for all the base lies
> That the almanacs hold,
> While there's love in the heart,
> We can never grow old.

> May fortune still be kind to you,
> And happiness be true to you,
> And life be long and good to you,
> Is the toast of all your friends to you.

> To friendship: May differences of opinion
> cement it.

Here's to cold nights, warm friends, and a good
drink to give them.

May your house always be too small to hold all
your friends.

Here's to our friends, and the strength to put up
with them.

Here's to friendship,
May it be reckoned,
Long as a lifetime,
Close as a second.

Friendship is the wine of life:
Let's drink of it and to it.

However rare true love is,
true friendship is rarer.

Don't walk in front of me,
I may not follow.
Don't walk behind me,
I may not lead.
Walk beside me,
And just be my friend.

Here's to a friend: He knows you well and likes
you just the same.

May the friends of our youth be the
companions of our old age.

The Lord gives us our relatives—thank God we
can choose our friends.

Here's to tall ships,
Here's to small ships,
Here's to all the ships in the sea.
But the best ships are friendships:
Here's to you and me!

May we have more and more friends, and need
them less and less.

Here's to you, old friend,
May you live 1,000 years,
Just to sort of cheer things up,
This vale of human tears.
And may I live 1,000, too—
A thousand, less one day,
'Cause I wouldn't care to be on earth,
And hear you'd passed away.

To our best friends, who know the worst about
us, but refuse to believe it.

May the hinges of friendship never rust,
nor the wings of love lose a feather.

May you have the strength to change those
things that can be changed,
May you have the patience to live with those
things that cannot be changed,
May you have the wisdom to know one from
the other!

To our friends: May the present have no
burdens for him/her and the future no terrors.

May good fortune precede you,
May love walk with you,
May good friends follow you.

Old friends are scarce,
New friends are few,
Here's hoping I find,
One of each in you.

To our friends: Whether absent by land or sea.

To friendship: May its bark never founder on the rocks of deception

To friendship: May its lamp ever be supplied by the oil of truth and fidelity.

Unselfish friendship: May we ever be able to serve a friend, and noble enough to conceal it.

To our friends: May we always have them and always know their value.

To our friends: May we be richer in their love than wealth, and yet money be plenty.

To careful kindness: May we never crack a joke or break a reputation.

Long life to our friends: May the chicken never be hatched that will scratch on their graves.

May we have more and more friends and need them less and less.

Chapter
8

Holiday and Special
Occasion Toasts

Holidays and special occasions are times when even the most estranged or "strange" families enjoy gathering together for celebration. It may reflect our fantasies about the warmth and the glow of the season, or it may simply be a following of tradition. Whenever a holiday brings people together, it is always time for a toast.

Thanksgiving

One of the most traditional and family-oriented holidays is Thanksgiving. People travel from all around the country so they can be together with their families on this day. What is interesting about Thanksgiving is how universal it is for anyone who is American. It is a time when we focus on what we have and not what we are missing in our lives. Toasts for giving thanks should be uplifting and can be humorous. Spiritual toasts and prayers of thanks are certainly appropriate. Try some of these:

> Like the goodness of the five loaves
> and two fishes,
> Which God divided among the 5,000 men,
> May the blessing of the King who so divided
> Be upon our share of this common meal.

> Be not forgetful to entertain strangers for
> thereby some have entertained angels
> unawares.
>
> —Hebrews 13:2

Here's to turkey,
Here's to pie,
Here's to scales
That make us cry.

Eat thy bread with joy, and drink thy wine with
a merry heart.

—Ecclesiastes 9:8

In the age of terrorism:

May we be happy and may our enemies always
know it.

Christmas

One of the most important aspects of Christmas is together-ness. Remembering the "reason for the season" is important, but focusing on each other and how much you mean to each other is a good basis for a Christmas toast. If you want your Christmas toast to be traditional, it is a good idea to keep it on the more reverent or serious side. This is a time for remember-ing not only your faith, but those who are less fortunate.

To my dear family and friends gathered here
among the gifts, the food, and the light of the
festive tree, there is no greater gift than what
you mean to me.

A toast to our good fortune,
A toast to our good cheer,
Blessings be upon us
That we gather here next year.

God bless us one and all.
   —Tiny Tim in Charles Dickens' *A Christmas*
                                    Carol

May we all be blessed with the spirit of the season.

Here's to wishing you all a Merry Christmas,
good cheer, and a prosperous New Year.

Underneath the mistletoe,
This is where our love will grow.
As your lips touch mine,
I will know a love divine.

New Year's Eve

The midnight toast to the New Year sets the tone for the year to come, so make it a good one. Make it one with well-wishing and optimism for endless possibilities.

To a new year filled with fun, laughter, and happiness.

Here's to wishes for a future where there is no
need for resolutions.

May the world be a place of peace as we gather
together again next year.

St. Valentine's Day

Any romantic toast can be adapted for St. Valentine's Day. If
you want to bring your date, spouse, or lover closer to you, if you
have intentions for dessert, it is advisable not to use a humorous
toast. Fill your St. Valentine's Day toast with "your eyes," "I can't
live without you," and "you are the only one for me," and you
should be in good shape. Women want romance! Men want it too.
This is a holiday for lovers. If you are on a date with someone who
is just a "filler" so you don't have to sit home alone, you can keep
your toast somewhat neutral. Don't get caught up in the moment
and make promises you don't plan to keep. It just isn't nice. If you
are friends and know that you are "filler" for each other, you can
have fun toasting each other and acknowledging the sorry state of
your personal affairs.

I drink to thine eyes,
Beacons so true,
My heart skips a beat,
When I am thinking of you.

To the love of my life, and the purpose of my
dreams.

May our life be filled with our true devotion to a
love that transcends time.

Easter

Easter Sunday is a religious occasion so toasts should focus
on the significance of the day. Common themes are rebirth or
toasts that refer to peace and love.

Mother's Day

Even though many people claim that this holiday was formed
by the greeting card companies, it has become a part of our culture. Woe to thee who forgets thy mother on Mother's Day. If
you think it doesn't matter, think again. A skipped Mother's Day
entitles you to a full year of guilt or more if your mother has a
long memory.

If you are gathered with family to honor your mother, your
toast should be filled with praise.

To our mother who survived anything we
dished out and lives to remind us of it.

Mother, you were always there when we needed
you, showing us grace under pressure, and an
endless supply of love and support.

When God created mothers, He blessed us with
the top of the line.

Memorial Day

This is a holiday that has a historic origin. It is a significant holiday to commemorate any soldier who been killed defending the freedom of our country. The holiday began officially following the Civil War in 1868 when then Commander in Chief of the Army of the Republic, John Logan, ordered that May 30 be a day to commemorate all who had fallen defending their country. Memorial Day became a tradition, which later became a legal holiday. Although it is a time for holiday fun, we should not forget what it really about. Here are some toasts to mark the day:

> We honor those people who have fought for the
> freedom we enjoy in our country, the United
> States of America, and pray that we will someday
> know peace.

> This is a day to commemorate those who have
> given their lives in all past wars and who fight for
> our freedom yet today. May they feel our love
> and our sorrow at their loss and our appreciation
> for the great sacrifice they made.

> May God comfort the souls of all mothers who
> have lost their sons and daughters to war.

> May we never forget the cost of war so we may
> always strive for peace.

> May we never forget the spirit of our soldiers
> and the courage they have shown. May they

always serve as an example to us and may we
carry on their legacy.

To our soldiers: May their souls find the peace
they so valiantly struggled to achieve.

Father's Day

Father's Day may not be wrought with as many guilt points as
Mother's Day, but fathers like to be remembered too. This is a
day when you can honor your father for all of the good things he
does, but a little loving humor can't hurt either, as long as you
show your appreciation.

To a great dad who taught me everything he
knows but fortunately not everything I know.

You were always there when I needed you and
you are there when I need you now, so could
you spare a few bucks? Just kidding.

To a great man who is someone to be admired, I
only hope that someday I can be considered half
the man you are.

Independence Day

Fireworks commemorate the "rockets red glare, and the bombs bursting in air as proof that our flag was still there." The Fourth of July is a day for recognizing our independence from British rule. It is a day for celebration and is one of the happiest celebrations of the year. It is a time for picnics, parades, and fireworks. Any toast with a patriotic undertone will do, but you might want to try this one:

> Oh say can you see?
> If you can, you need another beer.

Labor Day

Labor Day is not a day to recognize all women who have given birth, although most women would probably say that this is something that should be recognized and that Mother's Day does not even begin to make up for it. Labor day is, as its name implies, is when we honor all of those people who make this country great by working.

Mothers view this holiday as the day when they can breathe a sigh of relief as it spells the end of summer and the beginning of freedom as children board their buses back to school.

No matter which holiday you are really celebrating, it is an opportunity for family barbeques, picnics, and outdoor fun. You can certainly recognize the meaning behind the holiday, but when you toast, it is perfectly appropriate to recognize how much fun it is to be together. Here are some ideas:

> As we end the summer and look toward fall,
> may we carry the joy of sunshine into the days
> ahead.

Too much work and no vacation
Deserves at least a small libation.
So cheer my friends and raise your glasses
Work's the curse of the drinking classes.

Graduation

The most common graduation for which there is a family celebration is from high school. This is a rite of passage that reflects the end of childhood and the transition into the next chapter in life. If the graduate is older than 18 years and the law agrees (most areas declare 21 the legal drinking age), some alcohol is appreciated, especially by the parents. Any graduation toast is adaptable to other graduation events such as from college or from specialized training. If the graduation is from graduate school or a Ph.D. program, make sure there is a great deal of recognition of how difficult the work has been.

Leaving high school is a step into the "real world." May you always make your world a better place by the example you set for others to follow.

To the graduate: We have every faith that you will be able to follow your dreams, but don't forget those who knew you when.

As you try to forget everything you have learned, always remember how to learn and to think for yourself.

Remember these days of youth
as they move swiftly,
Enjoy them while you can
because someday you'll be 50.

To the graduate—in a class by him/herself.

To the graduate: We are proud of what you
have achieved and know you will always give us
reason to brag.

Bon Voyage

We toast people who are taking a vacation, particularly a
cruise, because we are truly jealous. We may also be concerned
about their safe return. But in this day of uncertainty, it is best to
keep it light. Making jokes about terrorists and being searched
by security are probably in poor taste, as are toasts regarding
sea sickness. Here are some ideas:

May your voyage be filled with adventure, good
food, and good shopping.

May your vacation be everything you dreamed
and more.

May you have a safe and wondrous adventure.

May you enjoy the blessings of travel and have
safe passage.

May your bon voyage be filled with laughter,
music, and all the food you could possibly eat.

To creating memories.

To a couple/person who deserves a vacation
and all the joy that life has to offer. Raise your
glass, drink champagne, but be careful not to
drink the water.

Moving

To a family of neighbors
Who surely will be missed.
After you move
We'll take you off our list.

May your new home give you as much pleasure
As your moving is giving us.

May your new home be blessed with good
feng shui.

May the key to your new door unlock
Many new blessings for you and yours.

May your troubles be less
And your blessings be more.
And nothing but happiness
Come through your door.

A house is not a home without family and
friendship. As our friends you are like family—
we love you and will surely miss you.

May your right hand always be stretched out in
friendship, but never in want.

Birth of a Baby

To you and your new baby. Your baby will
make your love stronger, days shorter, nights
longer, bankroll smaller. But as you remember
these days, they will be remembered as among
the best of your lives.

A new life begun,
Like father, like son.
Like one, like the other,
Like daughter, like mother.

Father of fathers, make me one,
A fit example for my son.

Grandchildren are gifts of God. It is God's way
of compensating us for growing old,
And for all that our children put us through.

Each baby is a universe, a gift that proves that
God believes that mankind is worthy of being
renewed.

Whenever a new life enters this world, the
angels rejoice, we are happy to share your joy
with you.

Chapter
9

All-Occasion
Toasts

There are some toasts that do not fit neatly into any one category—or at least we didn't agree on quite where to put them. If you find one you like, memorize it so you can impress someone at the spur of the moment. You never know when some additional charm might come in handy.

"Let us toast the fools; but for them the rest of us could not succeed."

—Mark Twain (1835-1910)

Fill high the goblet! Envious time steals, as we speak, our fleeting prime.

May you always distinguish between the weeds and the flowers.

"Early to rise and early to bed makes a man healthy but socially dead."

—Alan Hale, *They Drive by Night*

May our lives, like the leaves of the maple,
Grow more beautiful and fade.
May we say our farewells when it's time to go,
All smiling and unafraid.

Here's to the land we love and the love we land.

May your joys be as deep as the ocean, and your misfortunes as light as foam.

"May the force be with you."
—Sir Alec Guiness, *Star Wars*

May we keep a little of the fuel of youth to warm our body in old age.

"Live long and prosper."
—Leonard Nimoy, *Star Trek*

May you enter heaven late.

"Here's mud in your eye."
—The Three Stooges

"Here's looking at you kid."
—Humphrey Bogart, *Casablanca*

May your future be filled with wine and roses.

"To making it count."
> —Kate Winslet, *Titanic*

To the old, long life, and treasure. To the young, health, and pleasure.

Non corber indum illeitimie. (Latin: "Don't let the bastards get you down.")

May you be blessed with health, happiness, and good harvest.

"Here's to plain speaking and clear understanding."
> —Humphrey Bogart, *The Maltese Falcon*

"Here's mud in my throat."
> —Bob Hope, *Son of Paleface*

To better times and a speedy calm to the storms of life.

All of this has been a religious experience: a living hell.

"A toast, a toast, a toast to mother dollar and to papa dollar. And if you want to keep this old building and loan in business you'd better have a family real quick."

—James Stewart, *It's a Wonderful Life*

Let us make the glasses kiss; let us quench the sorrow ciders.

Come fill the bowl, each jolly soul;
Let Bacchus guide our revels;
Join the cup to lip, with "hip, hip, hip,"
And bury the blue devils.

"Here's to us, to apple trees, to cheese and wine and bread and life itself."

—Alan Alda, *The Four Seasons*

"A toast—Jedediah—to life on my terms.
These are the only terms anybody ever knows: his own."

—Orson Welles, *Citizen Kane*

Here's to thee my honest friend,
Wishing these hard times to mend.
Laugh and the world laughs with you;
Weep and it gives you the laugh anyway.

"Here's to the time when we were little girls and
no one asked us to marry."

—Joan Crawford, *Humoresque*

May poverty always be a day's march behind us.

May you never forget what is worth
remembering, or remember what is worth
forgetting.

"To the fountain of Trevi where hope can be
found for a penny."

—Dorothy McGuire,
Three Coins in the Fountain

May you be poor in misfortune
and rich in blessings.
May you be slow to make enemies
and quick to make friends.
But rich or poor, quick or slow, may you know
nothing but happiness from this day forward.

Call frequently,
Drink moderately,
Park friendly,
Pay today,
Trust tomorrow.

"Revenge is a dish that is best served cold."
—Ricardo Montalban,
Star Trek II: The Wrath of Khan

May the morning of prosperity shine on the evening of adversity.

"To the men we loved: the stinkers."
—Eve Arden, *Mildred Pierce*

"I keep my friends close but my enemies closer."
—Marlon Brando, *The Godfather*

May the sunshine of comfort dispel the clouds of despair.

May we ever be able to part with our troubles to advantage.

To all that gives you pleasure.

Here's to you and here's to me,
And here's to love and laughter.
I'll be true as long as you,
And not a minute after!

The right time and place is coming for you; don't
let it pass.

Ad multos annos—to many years!

A health to you, a wealth to you,
And the best that life can give to you.

Stay happy, my friends,
Hang easy and loose,
Gettin' rattlesnake-riled
Is just no use.

We'll think of all the friends we know,
and drink to all worth drinking to.

May you have warmth in your igloo, oil in your
lamp, and peace in your heart.

To days of ease and nights of pleasure.

Delicious nights to an ever virtuous heart.

Good day, good health, good cheer, good night!

Here's to beauty, wit, and wine.

I drink to the days that are.

It is best to rise from life as from the banquet, neither thirsty nor drunken.

To a full stomach, a full purse, and a full heart.

Love to one, friendship to many.

May our faults be written on the seashore, and every good action prove a wave to wash them out.

May the clouds in your life form only a background for a lovely sunset.

To blue skies and green lights.

May we all live in pleasure and die out of debt.

May we be happy and our enemies know it.

Here's to our guest:
Don't let him rest.
But keep his elbow bending.
It's time to drink—
There's time to think,
Tomorrow—when you're mending.

May we live respected and die regretted.

May we live to learn well, and learn to live well.

Good company, good wine, and good welcome
make good people.

May we never feel want, nor ever want feeling.

May your life be as beautiful as a summer day,
with just enough clouds to make you appreciate
the sunshine.

Here's to the riotous enjoyment of quiet
conscience.

'Tis hard to tell which is best:
Music, food, drink, or rest.

It's not so bad a world,
As some would like to make it;
But whether good or whether bad,
Depends on how you take it.

May our house always be too small to hold all
our friends.

So here is a slogan
That's sure to match,
There ain't no use itchin'
Unless you can scratch.

The ornament of a house is the guests who
frequent it.

Happy to share with you,
Such as we got,
The leaks in the roof
The soup in the pot.
You don't have to thank us,
Or laugh at our jokes,
Sit deep and come often,
You're one of the folks.

May love draw the curtain and friendship the
cork.

To health and happiness!

May your journey through life be guided by fair winds and calm seas.

May all your troubles be little ones.

May all your days be as happy as the ones before.

Here's to you as good as you are,
Here's to me as bad as I am.
As bad as I am, as good as you are,
I'm as good as you are as bad as I am.

A toast to the glorious mysteries of life.
To all that binds the family as one.
To mirth, merriment, mischief.
To dear friends, to youth,
To passion, to desire,
To pain, to tonight.

May you pluck the feathers from the bird of life and may they tickle your fancy!

May your troubles be like grandma's teeth:
few and far between!

May your boots never get dusty, and your guns
never get rusty.

May all your pleasures become habits, and all
your habits become legal.

Here's to bread; it makes the best toast!

Always walk with your faces toward the sun, so
the shadows will fall behind you.

Here's to every day that ends in "y."

Here's to the roof above: May it never fall in,
and may our friends gathered below it never
fall out!

To a placid life: May we never murmur without
cause, and never have cause to murmur.

May care be a stranger and serenity a familiar
friend to every honest heart.

May bad example never attract youthful minds.

May poverty never come to us without rich
compensations and hope of a speedy departure.

To everyone everywhere:
Be to your virtues a little kind,
And your faults a little blind.

Here's to my lips and here's to my toes,
Where many quarts and gallons goes!

May you have the hindsight
To know where you have been,
The foresight
To know where you are going,
And the insight
To know when you have gone too far.

"It's a reality of life that men are competitive.
And the most competitive games draw the most
competitive men. That's why they're there—to
compete. They know the rules and the
objectives when they get into the game. The
objective is to win—fairly, squarely, decently,
by the rules—but to win. And in truth, I've
never known a man worth his salt who, in the
long run, deep down in his heart, didn't
appreciate the grind and the discipline. There is
something in good men that really yearns for,
that needs, that demands, discipline and the
harsh reality of head to head combat. I don't
say these things because I believe in the brute
nature of man, nor that man must brutalize to
be combative. I believe in God. I believe in
human decency. But above all, I believe that
any man's finest hour, his greatest fulfillment to
all that he holds dear, is that moment when he
has worked his heart out in a good cause and
lies exhausted on the field of battle, victorious!"
        —Vince Lombardi, football coach

We're only here for a short time, but we're here
for a good time.

Health, love, money, and time to spend it.

To the chef: Good food, good meat—good
God, let's eat!

Iron is strong, but fire melts it.
Fire is strong, but water quenches it.
Water is strong, but the sun evaporates it.
The sun is strong, but clouds can cover it.
Clouds are strong, but wind can drive clouds away.
Wind is strong, but man can shut it out.
Man is strong, but fears cast him down.
Fear is strong, but sleep overcomes it.
Sleep is strong, but death is stronger.
But the strongest is kindness.
It survives death.

—paraphrased from the *Talmud*

Bite off more than you can chew,
Then chew it.
Plan more than you can do,
Then do it.
Point your arrow at a star,
Take your aim and there you are.
Arrange more time than you can spare,
Then spare it.
Take on more than you can bear,
Then bear it.
Plan your castle in the air,
Then build a ship to take you there.

May we never lose our bait when we fish for
compliments.

When there's love in the heart,
There will be beauty in the character.
When there is beauty in the character,
There will be harmony in the home.
When there is harmony in the home,
There will be order in the nation.
And when there is order in the nation,
There shall be peace in the world.

To laugh is to risk appearing the fool;
Laugh anyway.
To weep is to risk appearing sentimental;
Weep anyway.
To reach out for another is to risk involvement;
Get involved anyway.
To place your ideas and dreams before a crowd
is to risk their loss;
Share your ideas anyway, and dream anyway.
To love is to risk being loved in return;
Love anyway.
To live is to risk dying;
Live anyway.
To hope is to risk failure;
You must have hope anyway.

But risks must be taken. The greatest hazard in
life is to risk nothing and do nothing—you will
dull the spirit. You may avoid suffering and
sorrow, but cannot learn, feel, change, grow,
love, and live. Chained by your attitude, you
are a slave. You have forfeited freedom. Only
if you risk are you free.

Children Learn What They Live

If a child lives with criticism,
he learns to condemn.
If a child lives with hostility, he learns to fight.
If a child lives with ridicule, he learns to be shy.
If a child lives with encouragement,
he learns confidence.
If a child lives with shame,
he learns to feel guilty.
If a child lives with tolerance,
he learns to be patient.
If a child lives with praise,
he learns to appreciate.

Chapter
10

Irish Toasts

When you read Irish toasts, they make you feel like you can be included in the celebration, whatever your ancestry. They are warm, funny, sincere, and show a love of life overshadowed only by a love of good whiskey. We have included a disproportionate amount of Irish toasts in this book because we were able to find so many good ones. Whether it is St. Patrick's Day or any day of the year, you can find a toast from this list that should suit your occasion. Perhaps the best introduction to this section is to quote an Irish toast:

> There are only two kinds of people in the world:
> The Irish and those who wish they were.

> Here's to the health of all those that we love,
> Here's to the health of all those that love us,
> Here's to the health of all those that love
> them...
> That love those,
> That love them,
> That love those,
> That love us.

> May you get all your wishes but one
> So you always have something to strive for.

God speed the plow and bless the cornmow.

God invented whiskey so the Irish wouldn't rule
the world.

It's better to spend money
like there's no tomorrow,
than to spend tonight like there's no money.

Get on your knees and thank the Lord you're
on your feet.

May the enemies of Ireland never meet a
friend.

May your glasses ever be full.
May the roof over your head be always strong.
And may you be in heaven half an hour before
the devil knows you're dead.

Here's to long life and a merry one.
A quick death and an easy one.
A pretty girl and an honest one.
A cold beer—and another one!

An old Irish recipe for longevity:

> Leave the table hungry.
> Leave the bed sleepy.
> Leave the table thirsty.

> May the joys of today
> Be those of tomorrow.
> The goblets of life
> Hold no dregs of sorrow.

> Always remember to forget
> The things that made you sad.
> But never forget to remember
> The things that made you glad.

> Always remember to forget
> The friends that proved untrue.
> But never forget to remember
> Those who have stuck by you.

> Always remember to forget
> The troubles that passed away.
> But never forget to remember
> The blessings that come each day.

> May the blessings of each day
> Be the blessings you need most.

> May the luck of the Irish possess you.
> May the devil fly off with your worries.
> May God bless you forever and ever.

St. Patrick was a gentleman
Who through strategy and stealth
Drove all the snakes from Ireland.
Here's toasting to his health.
But not too many toastings
Lest you lose yourself,
And then forget the good St. Patrick
And see all those snakes again.

Here's to thee and me and aw' of us!
May we ne'er want naught, none of us!
Neither thee nor me nor anybody else,
Aw on is—nawn of us.

May you have:
No frost on your spuds,
No worms on your cabbage.
May your goat give plenty of milk.
And if you inherit a donkey,
May she be in foal.

May the luck of the Irish
Lead to happiest heights
And the highway you travel
Be lined with green lights.

May the strength of three be in your journey.

May brooks and trees and singing hills
join in the chorus too.
And every gentle wind that blows send
happiness to you.

May your heart be warm and happy
With the lilt of Irish laughter
Every day in every way
And forever and ever after.

May the face of every good news
And the back of every bad news
Be toward us.

May you have food and raiment,
A soft pillow for your head,
May you be 40 years in heaven
Before the devil knows you're dead.

May your right hand always be stretched out in
friendship and never in want.

Here's to a sweetheart, a bottle, and a friend.
The first beautiful, the second full, the last ever
faithful.

May the grass grow long on the road to hell for
want of use.

Here's that we may always have
A clean shirt,
A clean conscience,
And a punt in your pocket.

May I see you gray, and combing your
grandchildren's hair.

Bless you and yours
As well as the cottage you live in.
May the roof overhead be well-thatched
And those inside by well-matched.

May the hand of a friend
Always be near you,
And may God fill your heart
With gladness to cheer you.

May those who love us, love us,
And those that don't love us,
May God turn their hearts.
And if He doesn't turn their hearts
May he turn their ankles,
So we'll know them by their limping.

Merry met, and merry part,
I drink to thee with all my heart.

Here's to the fellow who smiles
When life runs along like a song.
And here's to the lad who can smile
When everything goes dead wrong.

"May you live all the days of your life."
—Jonathan Swift, Anglo-Irish writer

May the Good Lord take a liking to you...but not
too soon!

As you slide down the banister of life,
May the splinters never point the wrong way.

Here's to temperance supper,
With water glasses tall,
And coffee and tea to end with—
And me not there at all!

If you're lucky enough to be Irish... you're lucky
enough!

May the leprechauns be near you,
To spread good luck along your way.
And may all the Irish angels,
Smile upon you St. Patrick's Day.

May you live long, die happy, and rate a mansion
in heaven.

May your troubles be less
And your blessings be more.
And nothing but happiness
Come through your door.

Here's to you and yours
And to mine and ours.
And if mine and ours
Ever come across to you and yours,
I hope you and yours will do
As much for mine and ours
As mine and ours have done
For you and yours!

May the Lord keep you in His hand
And never close His fist too tight.

Mothers [fathers] hold their children's hands
for just a little while...And their hearts forever.

May your thoughts be as glad as the shamrocks.
May your heart be as light as a song.
May each day bring you bright hours,
That stay with you all year long.
For each petal on the shamrock
This brings a wish your way—
Good health, good luck, and happiness
For today and every day.

May the blessings of light be upon you,
Light without and light within.
And in all your comings and goings,
May you ever have a kindly greeting
From them you meet on the road.

Health and a long life to you.
Land without rent to you.
A child every year to you.
And if you can't go to heaven,
May you at least die in Ireland.

May you be poor in misfortune,
Rich in blessings,
Slow to make enemies,
And quick to make friends.
But rich or poor, quick or slow,
May you know nothing but happiness
From this day forward.

Here's to the four hinges of society.
May you fight, steal, lie, and drink.
When you fight,
may you fight for your country.
When you steal,
may you steal away from bad company.
When you lie,
may you lie at the side of your sweetheart.
And when you drink, may you drink with me.

"A journalist invents his lies,
and rams them down your throat.
So stay at home, and drink your beer,
and let the neighbors vote."
—William Butler Yeats, Irish poet

The health of all Ireland,
and the County of Mayo,
And when that much is dead,
May we still be on the go.

May peace and plenty be the first
To lift the latch on your door,
And happiness be guided to your home
By the candle of Christmas.

Wherever you go and whatever you do,
May the luck of the Irish be there with you.

Forsake not an old friend, for the new is not
comparable to him.
A new friend is a new wine: When it is old, thou
shalt drink it with pleasure.

May there be a fox on your fishing hook
And a hare on your bait,
And may you kill no fish
Until St. Brigid's Day.

Here's to beefsteak when you're hungry,
Whiskey when you're dry,
All the women you'll ever want,
And heaven when you die.

Who is a friend but someone to toast,
Someone to gibe, someone to roast.
My friends are the best friends
Loyal, willing and able.
Now let's get to drinking!
Glasses off the table!

May your neighbors respect you,
Trouble neglect you,
The angels protect you
And heaven accept you.

May you have warm words on a cold evening,
A full moon on a dark night,
And the road downhill all the way to your door.
Here's to your health and prosperity,
To you and all your posterity.
And them that doesn't drink with sincerity,
That they may be damned for eternity!

May the holy Saints be about your bed, and
about your board, from this time to the latter
end.

Like the goodness of the five loaves
and two fishes,
Which God divided among the five
thousand men,
May the blessing of the King who so divided
Be upon our share of this common meal.

May the Irish hills caress you.
May her lakes and rivers bless you.
May the luck of the Irish enfold you.
May the blessings of St. Patrick behold you.

May the saints protect you,
And sorrow neglect you,
And bad luck to the one
That doesn't respect you.

Chapter
11

International
Toasts

There are many ways in this world to say cheers. Although specific languages may have more extensive translations, the phrases we have included all basically mean cheers or some form of congratulations. If you choose to use an international toast, you might be wise to check out the exact pronunciation with someone from that country. Your goal is to appear worldly or generous for trying to involve yourself in another culture. You will be acting against your goal if your pronunciation turns cheers into "your mother has chicken feet."

Albanian:

Gëzuar! ("All good things to you.")

Se hetan. ("To your health.")

Nga mot gëzuar. ("Happiness for many years.")

Rrofsh sa malet.
("May you live as long as the hills.")

Te kini shendene.
("May you enjoy good health.")

Arabic:

Al salam alaycum. ("Peace be with you.")

B' ism Allah! ("In God's name.")

Fi sihtak! ("To your health.")

Kasak! ("In your honor.")

Sihatikom! ("To your health!")

Besehtak! ("To your health! Good luck!
Success! Happiness!")

Argentinean:

Salud! ("To your health!")

Armenian:

Genatzt

Australian:

Cheers!

Austrian:

Prosit! ("May it be to your health.")

Belgian:

Op uw gezonheid! ("To your health.")

Bolivian:

Salud! ("To your health.)

Brazilian:

Saúde! Viva! ("To your health.")

Chinese:

Yum sen! ("Drink to victory.")

Kan pei! ("Bottoms up!")

Czech/Slovak:

     Na Zdravi! ("Health to you.")

Danish:

     Skal! ("A salute to you.")

Dutch:

     Proost!

     Geluch!

     Op je gezondheid! ("To your health!")

Esperanto:

     Je zia sano!

Estonian:

     Tervist! ("Good health to you.")

     Parimat tulevikuks! ("Best for your future!")

Ethiopian:

     Letanachin! ("To your health!")

Farsi:

     Salumati!

Finnish:

Kippis! Terveydeksi! ("To your health.")

French:

A vortre santé! Santé! Chin!
("To your health.")

Je leve mon verre a votre sante.
("I raise my glass to your health!")

Ici a la ange avec un demander pour un diable!
Moi!
("Here's to an angel with a yearning for a devil!
Me!")

German:

Prosit! ("To health.")

Ofen warm, Bier kalt, Weib jung, Wein alt.
("Oven warm, beer cold, wife young,
wine old.")

Greek:

Eis Igian!

Stin ygia sou! ("To your health!")

Greenlandic:

Kasuguta!

Gypsy:

>May you live until a dead horse kicks you!

Hawaiian:

>Havoli maoli oe! ("To your happiness.")
>
>Kou ola kino! ("To your health!")
>
>Huapala! ("To my sweetheart!")

Hebrew:

>L'Chaim ("To life!")

Hungarian:

>Kedves egeszsegere!

Icelandic:

>Santanka nu!

Indian:

>Aap ki sehat ke liye! ("To your health.")

Indonesian:

>Selemat!

Irish:

Slante!

Italian:

A la salute!

Viva l'amor! ("Long live love!")

Cin-cin! ("All things good to you!")

Japanese:

Omedeto Gozaimasu! ("Congratulations.")

Kampai! Banzai! Campi! ("Bottoms up.")

Korean:

Gung bai! ("Bottoms up.")

Chu-kha-ham-ni-da! ("Congratulations!")

Lithuanian:

I sveikatas! ("To your health.")

Mexican:

Salud!

Moroccan:

Saha wa'afiab!

New Zealand:
Kia ora!

Norwegian:
Skal!

Pakistani:
Sanda bashi!

Philippine:
Mabuhay!

Polish:
Na zdrowie! ("To your health.")
Na zdrowie, azeby nasze dzieci mialy bogatych rodzicow!
("To our health—may our children have rich parents!")
Sto lot! ("Another 100 years.")

Portuguese:
A sua suade!
Saúde e gôzo! ("Health and enjoyment!")
A sua felicidade! ("To your happiness!")

Romanian:

Noroc! ("Good luck.")

Russian:

Budem zdorovy! ("Let's be healthy!")

S priyezdom! ("Happy arrival!")

S otyezdom! ("Happy journey!")

Do dna! ("Bottom's up!")

Za Zdorovie molodech!
("To the health of the young couple!")

Spanish:

Salud!

Salud, pesetas y amor...y tiempo para gozarlos!
("Health, money and love...and time to enjoy them!")

Salud y amor sin suegra!
("Health and love without a mother-in-law!")

Swedish:

Skal!

Thai:

Sawasdi!

Chai yo! ("To your health and well-being!")

Turkish:

Serefe!

Ukranian:

Na zdorovya! ("To your health!")

Welsh:

Iechyd da!

Yiddish:

Zol zon tzgezhint! ("To your good health.")

Mazel tov! ("Congratulations!")

Zulu:

Oogy wawa!

Chapter
12

Business and
Retirement Toasts

When giving a business or retirement toast, the most important thing to keep in mind is that in any business setting there is an invisible line between business and personal. As much as our work environments have become secondary or even primary homes to us, it is best not to let your guard down too much. There is the old expression, "Thou shalt not dip thy pen in company ink." This can also be described in another way that shall be referred to here only through innuendo it has to do with not performing bodily functions in the same place in which you take your meals. You get the point. So have fun toasting your boss for having a doubled bottom line, just don't make fun of his or her spouse. Retirement parties can be fun, but remember, you will be returning to work on Monday.

General Business Toasts

When you have finished your work
And the day is done,
It's time to kick up your heels
And have some fun.

As you negotiate the days of your life, may you always keep your leverage.

To our company visionary who delivers the profits.

To our most valuable player. You've helped us
have a winning team.

To our best idea man/woman, who sees beyond
the bottom line.

Congratulating sales force on high numbers:

Here's to all the work you do
To make this company great.
Without you we would be a plane without
an engine.
Let's soar through another great year.

Closing a deal:

Here's to the big deal—
And having a good meal.

Here's to all the last minute crunches.
Here's to all those business lunches.
When the going was the roughest,
That's the time you were your toughest.
We could never do this without you.

To good judgment: May opinion never float in
the sea of ignorance.

Successful suit: May we court and win all the Daughters of Fortune except the eldest—Miss Fortune.

To the future: When great men are honest and honest men are great.

May we live to learn well and learn to live well.

To our merchant: May he have good trade, well paid.

May the devil cut the toes of our foes
So that we know them by their limping.

Secretary's Day

On this day when we honor those who are the power behind the throne,
I want to share my appreciation for the wonderful work you do throughout the year.

We know that flowers are good but cash is better. Hope you liked your flowers.

Retirement Toasts

Here's to doing nothing at all
Relax, enjoy, and just have a ball.
When you're sitting at home
with nothing to do,
Think of us still at work.
We're doing that, too.

To a (man/woman) who has contributed greatly
to the success of this business. We know that
whatever you do you will touch the lives of those
around you.

Welcome to the next chapter in your life! May
your book of life have a happy ending.

Here's to Florida winters. *(Substitute
appropriate venues.)*

Remember when you have nothing to do,
That no one does that better than you.

To you: You did it...whatever it is.

May you rediscover the dreams of youth, and
apply the wisdom of experience.

May your retirement bring you all the joy you
have been wishing for and may you know
happiness all the days of your life.

May all that you have contributed to this
company pay off in fish and birdies.

To your retirement. May your "I'll do it
someday" become "no time like the present."

May your retirement years be filled with love,
life, and laughter.

In your retirement years, may your plans always
exceed your calendar space.

You have always set a good example for us.
May you now set the example of how to get the
most out of retirement.

Go for the gold in your golden years. You will
always be golden to us.

May your children figure out quickly that
retirement means "got a life."

Gardening, reading, golf, and fishing,
May you lead the life for which we have all
been wishing.

May your new life be as a river that is headed
out to sea. May each day be an adventure of
self-discovery.

Good-bye to you. As you walk this new road of
life remember those you've left behind.

Chapter
13

Spiritual Toasts

There are many occasions that lend themselves to religious or spiritual toasts. The important thing to remember is that you may have a mixture of many traditions at any one event.

If you know that the toastee has strong preferences for a particular path, you can have more leeway in choosing a toast that is more direct. For example, you can use Jesus in a toast if you know the toastee is a devout Christian. It is not appropriate for you to use a toast with the name of Jesus if *you* are a devout Christian but the toastee is of a different faith.

In this time we are a bit more willing to be open about spirituality. There are many toasts that use a more generic sense of spirituality as opposed to defining exactly what that means for any particular group. It is likely that a sincere spiritual toast will not only be well-received but will be uplifting for those sharing in it with you.

May the Lord love us, but not call us too soon.

Grandchildren are gifts of God.

Children are God's way of compensating us for growing old.

To the Great Unknown—who is waiting to do us a favor.

Eat thy bread with joy, and drink thy wine with a
merry heart.

—Ecclesiastes 9:10

Here's to Eternity: May we spend it in as good
company as this night finds us.

As the two of you now become one through this
holy marriage in witness of God, and all friends
here, may He bless you with Faith, Hope and
Charity:
Faith, to believe in God,
Hope, to love and support each other,
Charity, to remember and love each person
that touches your lives.

May you love your husband, and you love your
wife, like Jesus loves you both.

May the Lord, God be over all in your life, and
may each of you be first in one another's life so
you both will have a joyous and fulfilling
lifetime of oneness in our Lord.

Father of fathers, make me one,
A fit example for a son.

May you be truly happy by loving each other and
agreeing wholeheartedly with each other,
working together with one heart and mind and
purpose.

> —Adapted from Phillipians 2:2

Love each other as God loves you—
unconditionally.

May the Lord of all creation bless you and
become part of your daily lives. May the
perfect, selfless love He showed all of us be the
love you have for each other. May each of you
always seek to be the perfect mate, and in so
doing have the perfect mate. May those of us
who love you, love you as one, as you will
become.

He who is learned in books alone may know
how things ought to be, but he who reads men
learns how things are.

Here's to the guiding light of our congregation.

The imprudent man reflects upon what he has
said, the wise man upon what he is going to say.

May the great spirit guide your walk.

May you find the serenity of oneness.

To a loving soul: May all the goodness you have given to this world be sent back to you tenfold.

May you find the truth you seek, without ever forgetting the question.

May you reap what you sow.

"Never be afraid to trust an unknown future to a known God."

—Corrie Ten Boom

To charity: A link from the chain of gold that angels forge.

To virtue: May we have the wit to discover what is true and the fortitude to practice what is good.

To err is human, to forgive is divine.

To the noblest qualities: Charity without
ostentation and religion without bigotry.

To the man we love: He who thinks most good
and speaks least of his neighbors.

The deeds of men: The best interpreters of their
motives.

To charity: A mantle of heavenly weaving used to
cover the faults of our neighbors.

Charitable allowances: May our eyes be no
keener when we look upon the faults of others
than when we survey our own.

Where there is doubt, faith.
Where there is despair, hope.
Where there is darkness, light.
Where there is sadness, joy.
Oh Divine Master, grant that I might not so
much seek to be consoled as to console.
To be understood as to understand.
To be loved as to love.
It is in giving that we receive.
It is in pardoning that we are pardoned.
And it is in dying that we are born to eternal life.

Chapter
14

Weird and Unusual
Toasts

The following are toasts that you may never have the opportunity—or *chutzpah*—to give. Any situation can be ripe for a toast if you have the right attitude. Be lighthearted and full of fun and you will find toasting opportunities at every corner.

Toasting a second wedding:

Here's to the triumph of hope over experience.

Toasting a fourth wedding:

May your optimism be outweighed only by the terms of your prenup.

Toasting a cannibal wedding:

May the skin of your bum
Never cover a drum.

Toasting a successful sex-change operation:

Lipstick, blush, powder, and paint,
Made a former man be what he ain't.

Upon reaching oneness with the universe:

Ommmmmmm.

Graduating from rehab:

> On this day,
> The first of the rest,
> May you always feel proud
> You've done your best.

Upon being fired from a job:

> May your new shift bring you
> closer to fulfillment,
> And may you find a new path
> that is right for you.

For mothers when children return to school:

> God bless the little children
> And the joy to home they bring;
> Here's to having quiet moments
> On the day the school bells ring.

On initiation into a vampire cult:

> Blood is thicker than water.

A toast for men taking Viagra:

> Here's to the wisdom of age,
> The desires of youth,
> And an extension of your warranty.

On paying off your mortgage:

Here's to a house that lasts at least as long as
your mortgage did.

On a stock fraud investigation:

May whatever they discover be a boost to your
career and not a bust to your rear.

After a bankruptcy discharge:

It is better to eat herbs and fear no creditors,
Than eat meat and have to hide from them.

—Talmud

To a fat friend:

May your shadow never grow less.

Take this job and shove it:

As the years go by
and you seal your fate,
Your boss on your tail
saying never be late,
Drink to the fact
that now you have quit...
When the alarm goes off
you don't care about it.

New car:

> Here's to my car
> All shiny and new,
> If you so much as touch it,
> I'll have to kill you.

Vasectomy:

> To my husband who figured out how it happened
> and put a stop to it.
> May we have many good times together.

A toast to discontented citizens:

> May they speedily leave their country for their
> country's good.

When the boss or colleague you hate is leaving:

> May you bring to your new job all that you
> brought to us.
> And may they return the favor to you.

Shotgun wedding:

> To a couple who always believed in dessert
> before the meal.
> May your life be filled with joy and wonderful
> surprises.

75th high school reunion:

> I would like to give a cheer
> But I am the only one who is here.

Divorce:

> Here's some hair of the dog that bit you. We
> hope you got a good bite out of him.

> Here's to your freedom to start a new life or to
> do everything exactly the same way if you feel
> like it.

> May the new life before you fulfill the dreams
> you have always had for yourself.

> May this surprise twist to your fairytale mark a
> new and exciting chapter in your book of life.

> As one thing ends, new life can begin. May you
> find everything you are looking for.

> May your ex get everything he/she deserves.

Older woman younger man:

> Who cares if I'll need a nip and a tuck, I still look hot and he's a good...companion.

Bon voyage:

> As you begin your vacation may you be stricken with the kind of temporary amnesia that erases all memory of anything to do with "real life."

Conclusion

Whether you prefer tea, beer, or champagne, the act of proposing a toast has little to do with beverage and everything to do with festivity. With a toast you can honor someone, congratulate them, roast them, and chide them. You can propose, dispose (retirement), or let off steam. You can wish people well or you can wish people hell. The best thing about the art of toasting is that you have room to use your own unique style within the boundaries of decency and what will most protect you from a punch in the mouth. In other words if you choose your words wisely you can be the life of the party. If you plan to use your forum to vent frustrations, insult, or bring attention to yourself at the expense of the honoree, go back and read this book again.

We hope you were able to find the right toast for your occasion.

> Here's to the readers of toasts
> Who make our jobs worthwhile;
> Here's to the givers of toasts
> Who make their listeners smile.
> Here's to our book's publisher and editors
> Who gave this book a trial,
> And here's to royalty checks,
> We hope we earn a pile.

Write a Toast

These pages are for you to create your own special toasts. Although we have shown you examples of toasts for all occasions, you may have occasions we have yet to conceive. For that matter, the best toasts may have yet to be written. Who knows? Maybe the toast you write today will become a favorite saying of tomorrow. We know it will become a treasured memory for your family and friends.

_____

_____

_____

_____

_____

_____

_____

_____

AMAZING
TRUE
STORIES

AMAZING TRUE STORIES

Don L. Wulffson
Interior illustrations
by John R. Jones

SCHOLASTIC INC.
New York Toronto London Auckland Sydney

For Gwen, a very special young lady

ISBN 0-590-45958-9

12 11 10 9 8 7 6 5 4 3 2 1   3 4 5 6 7 8/9

Printed in the U.S.A.   28

First Scholastic printing, January 1994

CONTENTS

ACCIDENTS AND DISASTERS

ART AND LITERATURE

SCIENCE

POLITICS AND GOVERNMENT

THE UNKNOWN AND MYSTERIOUS

ALL IN SPORT

WEIRD WEATHER

Travel
and
Transportation

A Package for Grandma

In 1914, May Pierstorff's parents wanted to send their four-year-old daughter to visit her grandmother. But the Pierstorffs were poor. The price of an ordinary train ticket for the 100-mile trip to Lewiston, Idaho, was more than they could possibly afford. After much thinking, the Pierstorffs came up with a very cheap—and very unusual—way to transport their child.

They decided *to mail her* to her grandmother.

At the post office, the postmaster studied all the rules. Little May fit the weight requirements. She weighed 48 pounds; 50 was the limit. It was not legal to send live animals through the mail—except for baby chicks. The postmaster decided she fit the category. He listed her as a 48-pound baby chick! He collected 53 cents in postage from her parents, and glued the stamps to a tag on the little girl's coat.

May was driven to the depot and put into the mail baggage car. On her journey, she was under the care of the train baggageman. Arriving in Lewiston, she was taken to the post office. The custom was to leave packages there overnight. However, a kindly clerk made an exception. He stopped his work and made a special delivery of the little girl to her grandmother.

A Funny Thing Happened on the Way to . . .

Have you ever felt that some drivers on the road are a bit wacky, a bit confused? Does it look to you like the only place they're headed is into an accident?

Read some actual insurance accident reports. The writers were asked to describe very simply and very clearly what happened. Their writing skills turned out to be about as sharp as their driving skills . . .

> The guy was all over the road; I had to swerve a number of times before I hit him.

> I had been driving my car for 40 years, when I fell asleep at the wheel and had an accident.

> The telephone pole was approaching fast. I was attempting to swerve out of its path when it struck my front end.

> I was on my way to the doctor's with rear end trouble when my universal joint gave way causing me to have an accident.

An invisible car came out of nowhere, struck my vehicle, and vanished.

I saw the slow-moving sad-faced old gentleman as he bounced off the hood of my car.

Coming home, I drove into the wrong house and collided with a tree I don't have.

I was unable to stop in time and my car crashed into the other vehicle. The driver and passengers then left immediately for a vacation with injuries.

In my attempt to kill a fly, I drove into a telephone pole.

The pedestrian had no idea which direction to go, so I ran over him.

The indirect cause of this accident was a little guy in a small car with a big mouth.

I thought my window was down, but I found out it was up when I put my hand through it.

My car was legally parked as it backed into the other vehicle.

I was thrown from my car as it left the road. I was later found in a ditch by some stray cows.

The Man in the Flying Chair

Larry Walters, 33, lived in San Pedro, California. His girl friend lived over a hundred miles away, in a desert town. Larry wanted to go see her.

Nothing unusual about that. What *was* unusual was how Larry planned to get from San Pedro to the desert.

Larry rigged forty-two weather balloons to an aluminum lawn chair. He and a few friends pumped the balloons full of helium. He sat down in the chair. Larry gave a thumbs-up signal.

His friends slowly let out the lines that held the chair. Suddenly, one of the lines broke. The jolt caused the others to lose their grip. Larry shot upward.

"It kind of shocked me when it let go," he said later. "It knocked my glasses off. I couldn't see very well, and I was really going up fast."

In hardly any time at all he was at 16,000 feet. A startled jetliner pilot spotted him. He radioed back that "Some crazy guy just flew past in a chair!"

"That jet plane flashing past scared me," said Larry. "But the view was great. I had a camera along, but I didn't take

any pictures. Not one. I was too amazed by what I was seeing with my own eyes."

Larry had wanted to go all the way to his girl friend's house. But there was almost no wind. He was hardly moving along at all.

"I had gone only about 50 miles," said Larry. "I was over Long Beach. I knew I wasn't going to make it to the desert. But I wasn't even thinking about that anymore. I was getting scared, and it was cold. That was the worst thing. Especially my face and feet. They were freezing."

Ice-cold—and going almost nowhere—Larry had had enough. After almost two hours in the air, his only thoughts were of getting down alive.

"I was prepared," he said. "I had a pellet gun. I started shooting at the balloons. As each one popped, I'd go a little lower. After a while, I was gliding over streets and buildings and houses. That was the scariest part of all. I was sure I was going to crash into something and get killed. I was especially afraid my aluminum chair would hit the power lines, and I'd get electrocuted."

He almost did. In his chair, he floated under some power lines. The balloons caught on the wires, stopping him. He swung back and forth for a few minutes. Then he edged out of his chair—and dropped to the ground.

Safe and sound.

"You ever plan to do this again?" a reporter asked Larry later.

He laughed and shook his head. "It was something else," he said. "I'll never forget it. But it was a stupid thing to try. I'm just lucky to be alive."

Buddy-system Driving

A few years ago in Jackson, Mississippi, a policeman was on traffic patrol. He noticed a car that was zigzagging wildly through traffic. Flipping on his siren and lights, he went in pursuit. After a short chase, he brought the car to a halt.

Two men were seated in the car.

When the policeman asked the driver for his license, he explained that he had none. "I can't get a license," said the driver as he took off dark glasses. "Fact is, I'm blind," he added, turning his head in the general direction of the policeman.

"Then what in the world are you doing driving a car!" demanded the officer.

The blind man shrugged and pointed toward the man in the seat next to him. "My friend here is giving me directions. But he's plastered. He's way too drunk to drive by himself. He was doin' the seein' and I was doin' the steerin'. Pretty good idea, huh?"

The policeman didn't agree. He arrested both men and took them to jail.

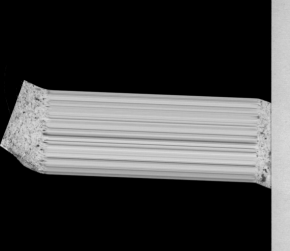

He Knew There Was Something He'd Forgotten

It happens to all of us. We return home from a vacation. Then we discover we left something behind.

That's what happened to Ken Zimmer. But his case is more unusual than most.

Over the Christmas holiday in 1988, Zimmer took his family on a trip to San Francisco. He and his wife and five children spent a week in the city. When the week was up, they headed for home in the family van. Home was Eugene, Oregon, several hundred miles north of San Francisco.

They drove all night. It was a long, tiring haul.

It was dawn when Zimmer finally pulled into the driveway of his home. That's when it hit him. That's when Zimmer realized he'd left something behind.

His wife!

About halfway home, they had stopped for something to eat. After they had eaten, Ken slid in behind the wheel. The others crawled into the back of the van. Ken headed out onto the highway—and was soon whizzing along. And everybody else was in the back of the van, settling down for a long snooze.

Everybody, that is, except Ken's wife, Pat.

She was running through the parking lot after the departing van. It disappeared into the darkness. She waited, knowing he'd soon realize she wasn't aboard.

He didn't, not until five hours later, as he pulled into his own driveway.

Worried sick, Ken filed a missing persons report with the police.

That afternoon, a call came. It was from his wife. She had taken a bus back to Eugene. She was at the bus station, and needed a lift.

Red-faced but relieved, Ken drove down to get her.

No Dogs Allowed

Thousands of people cross the Golden Gate Bridge, in and out of San Francisco, every day. To cross it, motorists have to stop at a toll booth and pay $1 or $2, depending on the day of the week. If a person does not have the money, he or she can leave something equal in value to the toll. The item is tagged. Then the owner can return later and pay the toll to get it back.

But sometimes the people don't come back. All sorts of strange items pile up.

Over the years, drivers have left the following items: a can of motor oil, a tool kit, rock 'n' roll cassettes, a set of silver tableware, a TV, men's wedding rings (these are left by the dozens), a set of false teeth, swim fins, a blouse, a frying pan, and a toilet plunger.

The most expensive item ever left was a $7,000 diamond wristwatch. Years passed. The owner still did not pick it up. Finally it was sold at auction for $5.

There are some things the toll officers cannot accept. People have tried to leave such things as uncanned food, their driver's license, even their eyeglasses. The strangest was a man who wanted to leave his dog. The toll booth operator settled for the collar.

Long-lost Stranger

In 1975, the Williams sisters went to the London airport to meet a long-lost brother. They drove home with a complete stranger.

"There he is!" they shouted as a nice-looking young man got off the plane. The sisters hugged him and smothered him with kisses.

Steve Stone of Buffalo, New York, was surprised. But he was also pleased at all the affection four pretty young women were showing him. "Gee, this is great!" he kept saying.

They hustled him off to their car. They even carried his suitcases for him.

"Are you this nice to everyone?" he said with a wink.

"No, silly, just the ones we love!" said one of the sisters.

"Well, this sure is great!" said Mr. Stone again as they drove off in the car.

"Well, it's great for us, too," said one of the sisters.

"It was such a hard thing," added another. "Us girls in England, and you bein' sent to live in America."

"Huh?" said Stone.

"Heavens, I was only twelve the last time I saw you," said another.

"What?" blurted Stone. "I've never seen any of you before in my life!"

The driver slammed on the brakes. A lot of explaining was done. Embarrassed, they drove back to the airport.

Stone wandered off to find a taxi.

In the lobby of the airport, the girls spotted a lonely looking young man. He was sitting by himself, wondering what had become of his long-lost sisters.

Crime
and
Punishment

Bad Break

In 1959, a man made a daring escape from a prison in Sydney, Australia. However, things did not work out exactly as he had planned.

The prisoner escaped by climbing underneath the hood of a van. The van was delivering bread to the prison.

He squeezed his body over and around the engine, then pulled the hood closed. It was a cramped, dirty, and hot hiding place. Still, the prisoner must have smiled when the van was started up and headed out through the prison gate.

After a short journey, the van came to a stop. Waiting until it sounded as if the coast were clear, the prisoner lifted the hood and crawled out of his dark, greasy hiding place. What he saw couldn't have made him very happy. The van was parked inside the yard of another prison just four miles from the first!

Two guards had already spotted him. Their guns were drawn. "Hold it right there!" yelled one of the guards.

Certainly, there was nowhere to run. The man hung his

head and raised his hands. Then he was taken to a cell.

The next morning the man was returned to his own prison—in a paddy wagon, not a bread truck.

The Worst Bank Robbers

Down through history, there have been many shrewd, brilliantly planned robberies. This is not the story of one of them.

In August, 1975, three men were on their way to rob a bank in Scotland. On their way into the bank, they got stuck in the revolving doors. People in the bank laughed. A smiling security guard, not knowing what they were up to, came and helped free them. After thanking him, the three robbers sheepishly left the building.

A few minutes later the men decided to try again. This time they were able to make their way into the bank without getting stuck. "OK, this is a bank robbery," said the gang leader nervously.

Everyone in the bank started laughing. Obviously, it was a joke. After all, weren't these the same three silly men who had just gotten stuck in the revolving doors?

The bank robbers were getting mad, and also embarrassed. "What's wrong with ya?" stuttered the leader. "This is for real. And we want ten thousand dollars!"

The head cashier could hardly control herself. She almost fell down laughing.

The robbers weren't getting anywhere. They wondered perhaps if they were asking too much. The gang leader lowered his demand to $1,000, then to $100, then to a dollar each.

At this point, everyone in the bank was howling with laughter.

Angry, one of the robbers pulled out a pistol. Then he jumped up on the counter to get everyone's attention. He stumbled and fell with a crash, breaking his leg.

The other two made their getaway. They pushed their way out through the revolving doors. But the door only went halfway. The two were pushing the wrong way. The door stuck, locking them inside.

By now, everyone believed the fools had actually been trying to rob the bank. The police were called. Everyone had one more good laugh as they were finally hauled away.

Grand Theft

———

One evening in Los Angeles, Mrs. H. Sharpe was taking her dog, Jonathan, for a walk. Mrs. Sharpe, as always, had brought along a pooper-scooper and a plastic bag to clean up after her dog.

The two had a long and pleasant walk. Jonathan had finished his business and Mrs. Sharpe had finished her cleanup. It was getting dark, and the two headed for home. Suddenly, Mrs. Sharpe heard a rustling noise behind her. Frightened, she hurried her pace. But in the next instant a shadowy figure rushed up from behind, snatched Mrs. Sharpe's bag from her hand, and raced off into the darkness.

It wasn't a handbag that the thief got. It was a plastic bag. And you *know* what was in that bag. One can only imagine the look on the thief's face when he looked in the bag to count his loot and discovered what he had stolen.

It would seem that this is one of those rare cases in which the criminal really got what he deserved.

In the Pen

THE YEAR: 1924. THE PLACE: Pike County, Pennsylvania.

Looking sad-eyed and a bit confused, the prisoner was led into the courtroom. Character witnesses took the stand and testified that the accused was usually well-mannered, fun-loving, and friendly.

But the evidence was clear. The prisoner had committed murder. More witnesses were called. They described the killing in detail. It was an open-and-shut case.

"Guilty!" thundered the judge.

The prisoner hung his head but said nothing. Then he was led away. He was loaded into a paddy wagon and taken to the state penitentiary. The sentence: life in prison.

In 1930, the prisoner died behind bars in the arms of a fellow inmate. Others looked on and wept as he passed away.

On the surface, this would seem to be an ordinary story, an ordinary case. It's not. In fact, it is one of the strangest criminal cases on record. Why? For one reason—the prisoner was a dog!

Pep was a black Labrador retriever. And Pep's crime: he

had killed the cat of the governor of Pennsylvania. The governor loved his cat as though it were a person, and he wanted its killer treated as though human.

The governor was also a judge. He demanded not only that Pep be tried for murder, but that he be tried in his own courtroom. As to a jury, there would be none. The judge would render the verdict. Pep didn't have a chance. The judge had already made up his mind what to do with the dog; and off to prison he went.

Fortunately, our story can end on a happy note. Pep was allowed to wander at will through the prison. When the other prisoners went out on work details, he trotted out with them and kept them company. Everybody liked him, and he liked everybody. He brought joy to his fellow inmates, and he was lavished with love until the day he died.

Icy Standoff

December 2, 1975, was a freezing cold day in Carson City, Nevada. Harold Hess, a local businessman, had just finished an errand. Making his way back to his car, he was annoyed to find a policeman writing him a parking ticket.

Hess went to the policeman. He explained that he didn't deserve a ticket. He had tried to put money in the parking meter, but it was frozen. Taking out a dime, he showed the policeman that the meter wouldn't work.

The policeman just shrugged. "That's not my problem," he said, handing Mr. Hess the ticket.

Though angry, Mr. Hess decided to pay the fine.

The following day he walked into the courthouse. After waiting his turn, he walked up to a justice of the peace. He smiled and presented the man with a large block of ice. In the center of the frozen block were the ticket and the money to pay the fine.

"Hey, how am I supposed to get that out of there?" demanded the justice of the peace.

Mr. Hess just shrugged. "That's not my problem," he said, and walked out of the room.

The Cop Who Became His Own Prisoner

The rookie police officer was nervous. It was his first day on the job. He had been assigned to traffic patrol.

Only a few minutes had passed before he spotted his first lawbreaker. A man driving a pickup truck breezed through a stop sign. After a brief chase, the officer gained the driver's attention and waved him to the side of the road.

The officer stepped from his car and locked the door. He had not taken two steps before he realized he had left his citation book in the car. Turning back, he discovered something far worse. He had locked his keys in the ignition!

The rookie gave the man in the pickup truck a warning and sent him on his way. He then walked back to the patrol car, climbed into the backseat, and tried to reach through the wire grill to unlock a front door. Just then a car whizzed by, and he slammed the back door to keep it from being hit—locking himself in the prisoner section! He used a portable walkie-talkie to call the chief of police to come and set him free.

A Lesson in Geography

It happened a few years ago in the town of Santa Fe, Argentina. A man boarded a local bus. He waited for everyone to take their seats. Then, gun in hand, he sneaked up behind the driver. "This is a hijacking!" said the man. "Take me to Cuba!"

"Didn't you ever go to school?" asked the driver.

"Huh?" said the hijacker.

"Well," said the driver, "I can't take you to Cuba."

"And why not?"

"Because Cuba is across the ocean. And this bus doesn't drive on water."

"Oh," said the man. "Guess you better let me off, then."

"No problem," said the driver as he opened the bus door.

The would-be hijacker, gun still in hand, got off the bus. Spotted by police, he was quickly arrested.

Killer Sues Prison

In 1979, Wally Weed murdered a young minister. He was convicted and sent to Utah State Prison for life.

On a summer day in 1984, Weed and two other men escaped from the prison. All three were captured a few days later.

When Weed was returned to prison, he filed a $2 million lawsuit. He sued the prison *for putting him in danger by letting him escape*!

"I was real afraid the whole time," he complained in the suit. "Mean cops with shotguns were after me. I had to swim through big streams. I got all scratched and bruised. I hurt real bad, and I was all hot and sweaty. Mosquitoes and other bugs bit me all over. It's only fair that they have to pay for what I went through. It's their fault I escaped."

Weed had another demand. He wanted the warden and all the prison guards fired. "They should be punished," he said, "for not doing their jobs very good."

To date, none of Weed's demands regarding the firing of prison personnel have been met. He's still waiting for the outcome of his lawsuit.

In the meantime, he has filed another one. In this suit he complains that he has been put in a cell by himself with a round-the-clock guard. This is unfair, he believes, regardless of the fact that he is in there to make sure he doesn't escape again.

Accidents
and
Disasters

Frozen Alive

It was an icy December morning in 1987. Nine-year-old Justin Bunker climbed from bed and glanced out at the snow-blanketed Connecticut countryside. He dressed, ate a quick breakfast, then made his way across the snow to a friend's house.

The two boys borrowed a sled from a neighbor. Then they headed to the playground of a nearby school. It had a great hill for sledding.

There was a shortcut into the playground. The chain link fence around an outdoor swimming pool had an opening in it. The boys climbed through. They were making their way around the iced-over pool, but it was just too tempting. Justin and his friend skated out onto the thick ice in their boots. The two began horsing around. That's when it happened.

Without warning, the ice gave way under Justin's feet. He let out a yell as he shot down into the freezing cold water. His friend watched helplessly. He stared down into the dark hole through which Justin had fallen. Justin appeared to be on the bottom, face-up and not moving.

41

In a state of panic, the boy raced to Justin's mother, who called the fire department. Within six minutes, firemen and paramedics arrived at the scene. Two of them immediately jumped into the frozen pool. Their heavy clothing and the darkness of the icy water made it hard to move rapidly. Several minutes passed before they reached the apparently lifeless body.

Finally, Justin was dragged from the pool. But there was no hope. He had been completely underwater for over twenty minutes. His eyes were frozen shut. His lungs and stomach were partly filled with ice-cold water. His body was stiff.

Justin was dead—almost.

Paramedics worked on him as they rushed him off in an ambulance. When he reached the hospital, he was unconscious and unable to breathe on his own. But he did have a faint pulse.

Doctors wrapped him in an electric heating pad. An oxygen mask was strapped over his face. For eight hours he lay in a hospital bed, unmoving, seemingly lifeless.

Suddenly he sat up in bed! Two nurses rushed to him. He pulled off the oxygen mask and tried to struggle free of the electric blanket. The nurses held his arms and tried to calm him. "Let go of me," he demanded. "What's going on? What happened?"

A few weeks later, Justin went home. He was healthy and normal in every way.

The obvious question is, how could someone be completely underwater for more than twenty minutes and still live? It seems impossible, but the same thing has happened to quite a few people. Justin's case is simply one of the most dramatic ones.

When someone plunges into freezing water, he or she may be "quick-frozen." Blood vessels near the skin shut down. The brain and other organs cool rapidly and need very little oxygen. The heart beats very slowly, and may even stop. Basically, the person is in a state of suspended animation.

That is what happened to Justin Bunker. And that is why he is alive and well today.

Fall Out, Fall In

On a September day in 1918, two Canadian airmen were on a training mission. At the controls of the open-cockpit biplane was George Makepiece. His passenger was Captain J. H. Sedley. Neither man wore a parachute or seat belt.

Pilot Makepiece cruised at a high altitude for a time. Suddenly he went into a steep dive. In the process, Sedley fell out of the plane.

Makepiece brought the plane out of its dive and leveled off several hundred feet below. High above, he could see Sedley free-falling. There was nothing the pilot could do. Sedley was falling to his death.

Makepiece lost sight of the man. Suddenly he was startled by a loud thump near the tail of the plane. He looked back and was shocked to see Sedley! Somehow the falling man had landed back on the plane!

For several minutes Sedley held on for dear life. Then slowly he climbed back into his seat.

A short time later the plane landed safely. Both men were speechless but unhurt.

A Favor Returned

It was a summer day in 1965. Four-year-old Roger Lausier was having a grand time. His parents had taken him to a beach near Salem, Massachusetts. He made sand castles. Then he waded out into the water. There was a sudden drop-off in the footing below, and little Roger was suddenly over his head. He didn't know how to swim. He tried to cry out, and sucked water into his lungs.

The little boy knew he was drowning. But a moment later, strong arms were around him. Then a woman was carrying him to shore.

Roger's mother was crying. Both she and her husband blamed themselves for taking their eyes off their son—if only for an instant. They thanked the woman again and again.

Her name was Alice Blaise.

Nine years later Roger returned to the same beach. He was now thirteen. He was big and strong for his age, and a good swimmer.

Spreading his towel on the sand, he suddenly heard a

shout. It was a cry for help. Beyond the breakers he could see a man fighting for his life.

Roger grabbed an air raft and quickly paddled out to the man. He reached him not a moment too soon. Roger helped the man onto the raft. Then, sliding into the water, he towed him to shore.

Later, Roger learned something very interesting about the man. His last name was Blaise. His wife was Alice— Alice Blaise, the woman who had saved Roger from drowning nine years before on the exact same beach.

Tidal Wave!

It happened in north Boston, on January 15, 1919. It was a few minutes after noon. No one had any idea of what was coming their way.

Workers were busy down by the docks and in warehouses. Horse-drawn carts clattered through the streets. Model T Fords chugged along, hooted horns. People strolled.

It hit suddenly, with almost no warning. There was a deep rumbling noise. Then a tidal wave two stories high slammed into the city.

Houses and buildings shattered. The Boston Fire Station was lifted from its foundation. Firemen were crushed and drowned as the station crashed into the harbor.

At a park, many workers had just settled down to eat lunch. Some never even saw the wave coming. They drowned where they sat.

An elevated train track collapsed. Train cars were picked up and thrown about like toys.

Neither horses, cars, nor people on foot could outrun the monster wave. It caught up to them, swallowed them up, carried them away.

In all, 21 persons died and more than 150 were in-jured—by the strangest tidal wave in history.

It was not a wave of water.

At the Purity Distilling Company a huge cast-iron tank had rumbled its low warning. Then it had burst open, releasing a great wave of raw black *molasses*!

Two million gallons of the sweet, sticky syrup had swept through north Boston. Sightseers who came later couldn't help but walk in the stuff. On their way home they tracked the goo throughout the city. Boston smelled of molasses for weeks. The harbor ran brown until summer.

A Miracle

It was the night of July 25, 1956. Slender, brown-haired, 14-year-old Linda Morgan was on board the passenger liner *Andrea Doria*, which was headed from Italy to New York. After dinner and a walk with her mother, Linda decided to turn in early. She made her way to her cabin, changed into her nightgown, and was soon fast asleep in her bunk.

Linda could not have known it, but bearing down on the *Andrea Doria* in the fog was the Swedish liner *Stockholm*. At the last moment, the captains of the ships tried to steer away from each other. It was too late. The *Stockholm* rammed into the *Andrea Doria*, tearing a 40-foot gash in its side.

The bow of the *Stockholm* sliced right through Linda Morgan's cabin. Nothing was left of it. The ship stopped. Then it went into reverse, pulling its bow out of the side of the *Andrea Doria*.

Hours passed.

The *Andrea Doria* was sinking. Its passengers were being rescued. The bow of the *Stockholm* was crushed, but the ship was still seaworthy.

Bernabé Garcia, a sailor aboard the *Stockholm*, was checking the damage to the bow. Suddenly he heard a cry for help. He made his way through the wreckage. He found a teenage girl. She was in a smashed bed on a mattress.

"What is your name?" asked Garcia.

"Linda Morgan," was the reply. "Where am I? What ship is this? What's going on?"

It was a while before anyone was able to figure out what had happened. The bow of the *Stockholm* had ripped into Linda's cabin, directly under her bunk. She was knocked out by a blow to the head. Then the ship had pulled back. As it did, it carried Linda, still in her bed, back out with it. Hours later she awoke on the bow of the *Stockholm*, miles away from the sinking *Andrea Doria*.

Linda was later taken to a hospital. She had three broken bones and other injuries, but she was going to be okay. Bernabé Garcia, who had first found her, came to visit. He smiled and touched her on the cheek. "It is a miracle," he whispered. "A miracle."

Art
and
Literature

Baseball Wasn't His Thing

"Take me out to the ball game,
Take me out with the crowd,
Buy me some peanuts and Cracker Jacks,
I don't care if I never get back."

Songwriter Jack Norworth wrote the greatly popular "Take Me Out to the Ball Game" in 1908. Incredibly, he didn't see his first baseball game till thirty-four years later, in 1942!

Norworth was on a New York City subway train when he spotted an ad for the old New York Giants baseball team. He found a pencil and a scrap of paper in his pocket and started scribbling. Thirty minutes later he'd finished the song.

In later years, Norworth joked that he had written "more than 3,000 songs, seven of them good." His big hits included not only "Take Me Out to the Ball Game," but also "Shine on Harvest Moon" and "Meet Me in Apple Blossom Time."

But how come Norworth had written such a famous song

about "America's favorite pastime" but had taken so long to be taken out to a ball game? When asked the question, he said, "So what? I'm a songwriter. That's what I like to do. Going to baseball games doesn't interest me a bit."

The E-less Novel

E is the most often used letter in the English language. In fact, *E* appears in so many words that it is difficult to write even one sentence without using one.

In Britain in 1939 author Ernest Vincent Wright published a novel entitled *Gadsby*. The strange thing about the book is that it is *E*-less. It has more than 50,000 words, none of which contains an *E*.

Surprisingly, *Gadsby* reads smoothly and well. The *E*s are hardly missed. Here is a sample passage from the work:

> Gadsby was walking back from a visit down in Branton on a Saturday night. Coming to Broadway, a booming bass drum and sounds of singing told of a small Salvation Army unit carrying on amidst Broadway's night shopping crowds.

Writing an E-less book must have been very hard. And the author did a good job. The only question is, why did he do it? What made him want to do something so odd? Perhaps the answer is simple. Maybe he just wanted to find out for himself if it could be done.

The Longest Painting

In the nineteenth century, artist John Banvard decided to do a painting of the Mississippi River. The result was not something you could hang on your wall. It was three miles long!

Banvard worked for years on the painting. In 1845, it was finally finished and put on display in Louisville, Kentucky. It was exhibited like a giant scroll. Showing scenes from along the Mississippi, it was unrolled from one huge spindle to another.

Banvard took his painting on tour throughout the United States and England. It is said that it was not an especially good painting, but people enjoyed it. The tours made Banvard a small fortune.

When the artist died, the painting was cut into sections. For many years, parts of it were used as backdrops in theaters.

Portrait of Death

Andre Marcellin was a painter who began work in 1907 in Paris. He did beautiful landscapes. People would often ask him to do portraits. Always, he would refuse. "I do not know why," he would say, "but for some reason I am afraid to do them."

A Paris banker kept after Marcellin. Finally, he got the artist to agree to do his portrait. Proudly, the banker sat as Marcellin worked.

Two days after the portrait was finished, the banker died.

Marcellin did not paint another portrait for six months. Then he felt the need to do another. A woman came to him and asked to have her picture done.

Again, two days later, the woman was dead.

It must be coincidence, Marcellin told himself. Wanting to prove this, he painted the likeness of another client. The man was a close friend.

The portrait was finished and paid for. The friend took it home.

Two days passed. Nothing happened. Marcellin breathed a sigh of relief. On the third day came the news. Marcellin's

friend had died that morning, suddenly and unexpectedly.

Marcellin was sure now that his paintings were cursed. He vowed never to paint another portrait.

For five years he kept good his vow.

In 1913, he met a lovely woman, Francois Noel. The two became engaged. Francois begged him to do her portrait. Marcellin refused. He told her of the curse. She laughed and said it was nothing but foolishness. Still, he refused.

As the months passed, Francois kept pestering him to do a painting of her. Everyday she became more and more angry. Finally, she told him he had to do her portrait. If he did not, then she would not marry him.

Marcellin gave in. He did the portrait. A week later, Francois died.

Marcellin was filled with sadness and guilt. For weeks he sat alone in his studio, doing nothing. Finally, he made a decision. He started work on another picture.

This one was of himself.

A few days after it was finished, Andre Marcellin was dead.

The $5,216 Fine
for an Overdue
Book

It was a spring day in the year 1984. Sixty-five-year-old Chet Hanchett quietly entered the Modesto High School library. Sheepishly, he made his way to the librarian's desk.

"I have a book to return," he said. "I'm afraid it's a bit overdue."

"How many days?" asked the woman.

"Not days—*years*," said Mr. Hanchett, placing a copy of Robert Louis Stevenson's *Kidnapped* on the desk.

The librarian opened the book. "Good heavens!" she said. "This book was checked out in 1934! It's fifty years overdue!"

Mr. Hanchett nodded.

The librarian went to work with a pocket calculator. When all was added up, the overdue fine came to $5,216.

Mr. Hanchett then said he found the book high up on a shelf. He had no idea as to how it came to be there. The last person listed as having checked it out was a high school friend.

The librarian smiled. She told Mr. Hanchett to forget the fine, and thanked him for returning the book.

A Book That Foretold the Future

In 1898, an English author named Morgan Robertson published a novel about a huge new ocean liner. The ship was far larger than any that had ever been built. The fictional characters on board were mostly the rich and famous. The ship set off on its first voyage. Halfway across the Atlantic, on a cold night in April, the make-believe ship hit an iceberg and sank. There was great loss of life.

Robertson's book, entitled *Futility*, did not do well. Few people read it. Few people even knew about it.

Certainly not the owners of the White Star Shipping Line.

Fourteen years after the publication of the book, White Star built what was then the largest ocean liner in the world. In nearly every way, it was almost exactly like the one in Robertson's novel. Both were around 800 feet long and weighed between 60 and 70 thousand tons. Both vessels had triple propellers and could make 24 to 25 knots. Both could carry about 3,000 people, and both had enough lifeboats for only a fraction of this number. But, then, this wasn't supposed to matter; both ships were said to be "unsinkable."

On April 10, 1912, the real ship left England on her first voyage. On board were some of the richest and most famous people in the world. On a cold April night, about halfway across the Atlantic, the ship struck an iceberg. With great loss of life, she sank.

The real ship, of course, was the *Titanic*. As for the name of the imaginary ship, the author called it the *Titan*.

Science

How Many Hours in a Day?

Everyone knows there are 24 hours in a day. But scientists say that days will be much longer in the future.

Ten billion years from now the length of a day on earth will increase from 24 hours to 564 hours! And 20 billion years from now a day will be at least 1,128 hours long.

Scientists say it is the force of the ocean tides that will make the days longer. Tides are gradually slowing the rotation of the earth. The more slowly the earth turns, the longer the days become.

Scientists also say that one of our days at present is six times longer than a day was when the earth was first formed. Though it may be hard to believe, a day on earth was originally only four hours long!

Frog in a Rock

On February 2, 1958, four men were at work in a mine in Utah. They hacked their way through eight feet of sandstone, then they came up against a fossilized tree trunk. The only way they could break it up and get it out of the way was by blasting.

The explosion cracked open the rock-hard trunk. The men went to carry away the broken slabs and pieces—and got the biggest surprise of their lives. In the center of the fossilized wood was a smoothly rounded hole about the size of an egg. And inside the hole was a tiny frog. It was shriveled and grayish-brown. Its toes were long but not webbed, and there were tiny suction cups on the ends of its fingers.

The creature lived for 28 hours after being released from the stony prison that had held it for ages.

Scientists studied the frog. No other like it was on earth. However, it was quite possible, they said, that such a frog had existed in prehistoric times.

But how did the frog come to be inside the rounded hole? It could not have crawled in through fossilized wood.

There were no gaps of any kind leading into the hole. It was a tightly sealed compartment.

To the scientists, the frog seemed to be a prehistoric creature. And it looked as old and dried up as the tree in which it was found, as though it had been trapped in there for centuries. But if so, then how could it still be alive?

It is one of the strangest cases in the history of science. So far, no one has been able to explain it.

The Human Radio

He thought he was going crazy.

Not long ago in Bridgeport, Connecticut, a factory worker was sure he was losing his mind. Everyday for weeks, he kept hearing music and little voices in his head. No matter where he went, the voices and music would follow him. He would even hear them in his sleep.

The man went to a doctor. It took a while, but the doctor found the problem.

A few weeks before, the man had had some dental work done. Accidentally, several little chunks of silver had gotten stuck between his teeth. The silver particles were picking up radio signals. The signals were then sent through the bones of his face to his brain. In effect, the man had been turned into a human radio receiver.

The doctor removed the bits of silver, and the man was cured.

A Comical Idea

One day in 1964, a freighter was entering the harbor of Kuwait. On board were 6,000 sheep. The ship was having problems. It was taking on water. Suddenly, it flipped over and sank.

Most of the crew escaped. All of the sheep went down with the ship.

The people living near the harbor were worried. Trapped inside the ship were thousands of sheep. As they rotted, the harbor would become badly polluted. The smell would be terrible.

A Danish man by the name of Karl Kroyer happened to be in town. Kroyer was not an engineer. But he did have an idea as to how to raise the ship.

At first, everybody thought his idea was silly. Kroyer suggested filling the inside of the ship with Ping-Pong balls. The air in them, he believed, would bring up the sunken freighter.

No one had a better idea.

A ship was sent to Kuwait Harbor. It carried 30 *billion* specially made plastic balls. They were like Ping-Pong balls, only much smaller, about the size of large pearls. The ship was also armed with a long injector hose. Divers took the hose down to the sunken freighter and injected the balls into the hull. At first, nothing happened. Then slowly but surely, the freighter rose to the surface.

Everyone thought Kroyer was a genius. It was such a great idea! How had he thought of it?

Kroyer laughed. Then he explained where the idea had come from. As a boy, he had loved comic books. One of those he had never forgotten was a Donald Duck story. In the story, Donald is on a boat with his nephews Huey, Dewey, and Louie. When the boat sinks, Donald and his nephews raise it, using Ping-Pong balls.

It had only been a silly, funny idea in a comic book. Funnily enough, the idea worked in real life—just as it had on paper for a bunch of make-believe ducks.

The Woman Who Couldn't Sleep

Like most people, you sleep about eight hours a day. In a year, then, you sleep 2,920 hours, and in thirty years, this comes to a staggering 87,600 hours!

For Mrs. Ines Fernandez of Seville, Spain, things were different. For the last thirty years or more of her life, she *never* slept—not for even an hour!

It all started on a warm summer afternoon long ago.

Mrs. Fernandez and her two children were standing in the open doorway of their house. A parade was going by. The children were jumping up and down with excitement. Mrs. Fernandez was a bit tired and bored.

"I yawned," said the woman. "And suddenly a horrible pain went through my head. Within a few hours the pain was gone. That night I went to bed, but I couldn't sleep. The next night the same thing happened. And the next, and the next, and the next. I've been that way ever since. I can rest, but I can never fall asleep. For over thirty years this has gone on."

Mrs. Fernandez went to many doctors. She took, she said, "thousands of pills." But neither the doctors nor the pills were of any help. Nothing could put her to sleep.

All in all, for the last thirty years or so of her life, Mrs. Fernandez was in good health. But she was always tired. "I am so tired," she would complain. "So very, very tired."

Each night, Ines Fernandez would put on a nightgown. But she had long ago given up on going to bed. Instead, she would sit down in a chair. And there she would wait— not for sleep, but for morning to come.

After more than thirty years of this strange torture, Mrs. Fernandez passed away. At long last, the sleepless woman was laid to rest.

Politics
and
Government

The Foot Powder Mayor

The year was 1969. The town of Picoaza, Ecuador, had a rather unusual problem. The town council was embarrassed. They didn't know what to do. The people had just elected a new mayor—one that came in a can.

The new mayor of Picoaza was a brand of foot powder! This is how it happened.

The Pulvapies foot powder company decided to make the most of an upcoming election. It ran ads that sounded like their product was a person running for office. The ads were the same size, shape, and color of real ballots. Across the top were the words, VOTE FOR PULVAPIES.

The votes were counted. To everyone's surprise, Pulvapies had won by a landslide! A foot powder was the new mayor!

Red-faced election officials explained to the people what had happened. Then they got a court order to keep the foot powder mayor from being installed in office. Finally, new elections were held.

A man won.

He wasn't very popular. In fact, he wasn't liked at all.
Signs began appearing. BRING BACK PULVAPIES! they read.
PULVAPIES, THE BEST MAYOR WE EVER HAD!

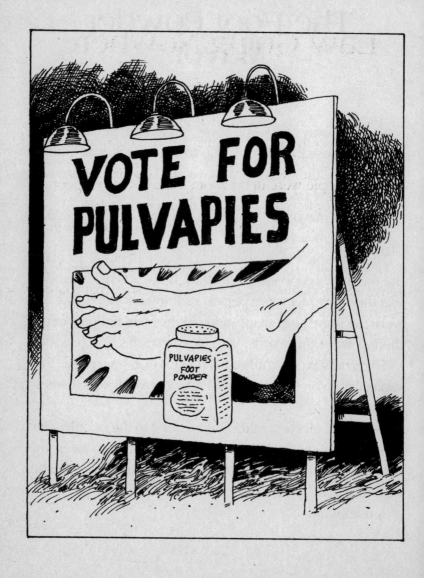

Law Going Nowhere

In 1971, the town leaders of Harbor Springs, Michigan, voted to lower the age for cab drivers. The age requirement was dropped from 21 to 18.

Many people were upset about the law, but not because younger people would be able to drive taxicabs.

"It's the silliest thing I've ever heard of," said one man. "The law just doesn't make any sense."

He was right. Lowering the age for taxi drivers made no sense at all. Why? For the simple reason that Harbor Springs lacked something. It didn't have any taxis. Not one.

The Do-nothing Congressman

The year was 1868. Thaddeus Stevens from Pennsylvania had been nominated by the Republican Party to run for office.

Republicans, of course, hoped Stevens would win.

The Democrats, naturally, wanted him to lose. In fact, they were especially nasty about Stevens' nomination. They said nominating him was stupid. He was a joke. He couldn't possibly do the job.

In November, the election was held. Stevens won by a landslide.

As it turned out, the Democrats were right about Stevens. He wasn't much of a Congressman. He never made any speeches. He wasn't on any committees. In fact, not once did he even show up for a congressional session!

Of course, no one expected him to. Not even the Republicans were surprised at Stevens' conduct. After all, they had only nominated him because they liked him, not because they thought he would do a good job. And how could he?

He was dead!

Thaddeus Stevens had long been a respected politician. In August, 1868, he died. Soon after his burial, he was nominated by his party as a "fitting tribute" to his memory. Three months later he was elected.

And for the next two years the United States had a dead Congressman.

Señor Banana

In 1974, Señor José Ramon del Cuet threw in the towel as mayor of the little town of Coacaloco, Mexico. Señor Cuet had a little help in making his decision. Four thousand citizens made it very clear they wanted him to go.

The people of Coacaloco made their living raising bananas. For years, the mayor had been lining his pockets. Large sums of money coming in from banana sales kept disappearing. The people got poorer and poorer. Señor Cuet got richer and richer.

Finally, the people were fed up. Four thousand strong, they stormed the town hall. Running from room to room, they finally found the mayor. He was hiding under a desk.

They pulled him out and sat him down. They demanded that he resign.

He refused. He said he was a good man, an innocent man. "Please, my friends, believe me."

A box of bananas was brought in. Then, one after the other, Mayor Cuet was forced to eat them.

Even a man who loves bananas has his limit. Finally, Cuet reached his. After all, twelve pounds of bananas *is* a lot to swallow.

Not feeling his best, Mayor Cuet took pen in hand and signed his resignation. Then he staggered away, out of the banana business forever.

King Henry I of America

Imagine opening a U.S. history book, and our first president isn't mentioned. But there *is* a lot about our *first king*—King Henry I of America!

The United States, of course, has never had a king. But we almost did.

It happened like this.

In 1783, the Revolutionary War came to an end. The colonies had finally won their freedom from British rule. What the new nation needed was a leader. But who should this person be? No one was sure. Debate on the question went on and on.

Three years passed. Still, no decision had been made.

Finally, a group of American statesmen got together. In the group were Alexander Hamilton, James Monroe, and Nathaniel Gorham. After many days of discussion, it was decided that what the United States needed was a king. And this man, they agreed, should come from one of the royal families of Europe.

Several names were brought up. After all had been discussed, it was decided that 50-year-old Prince Henry of

KING OF

THE UNITED STATES OF AMERICA

Prussia was the best man for the job. A few days later they sent him a long letter. It asked that he become "King of the American Colonies."

At first, Henry was excited about the idea. Then he had second thoughts. He wasn't sure he wanted to leave Europe or take a chance on being the ruler of such a wild and unsettled land. Then he changed his mind again. He sat down to write a letter accepting the offer.

He tore up the letter. He wanted more time to think.

Months passed. Finally, Henry did send off a letter. But all it said was that he wasn't quite sure what he wanted to do.

The letter not only annoyed the Americans, it also caused *them* to have second thoughts. What kind of a leader would Henry make? Did they really want a king who couldn't even decide whether or not he wanted to be king?

After more thinking and talking, everyone agreed to forget not only about Henry but also about having a king. Instead, there would be an elected president.

The rest is history.

But what if Prince Henry had said yes to the offer? If he had, all of U.S. history would be changed. Today, instead of an elected president, the country would be ruled by a king or queen, the descendant of a now-forgotten prince who had trouble making up his mind.

The Unknown
and
Mysterious

Into Thin Air

_____

It was the morning of September 23, 1880. On a small farm in Tennessee, David Lang and his wife were sitting on their porch. Their two children, George, 8, and Sarah, 11, were playing in the yard.

David Lang spotted two friends driving toward the farm in a buggy. He waved and headed across an open field to greet them. Suddenly he looked back at his family. Something was wrong. He seemed confused and in pain.

That's when it happened.

Standing in the middle of an open field, David Lang vanished into thin air!

His family and two friends rushed to the spot. They thought perhaps he had fallen into a hole or a crack in the ground. But there were none. The spot was nothing but flat, solid land. Sobbing and screaming, Mrs. Lang was led back to the house.

The sheriff came. Neighbors came. Dozens of people searched the field and nearby land. Even scientists were called in. They studied the area but could find nothing to explain what had happened. David Lang was simply gone.

For months the search went on. Curiosity seekers came to gawk. All the Lang servants and farmhands quit in fear.

When spring came, another strange thing happened. The grass in the spot where Lang had disappeared grew in a tall circle of green. The farm animals were afraid of the place. Not one of them would enter the circle.

One day in August, 1881, Lang's two children approached the circle of high grass. Sarah called out, "Father, where are you?" There was no answer. She repeated the question several more times. They were about to walk away. Suddenly they heard a faint cry. It was a cry for help that came from nowhere.

Quickly the children ran and got their mother. She returned with them to the spot. Mrs. Lang called out as the children had done. *Her husband answered!* For several days the family returned. Each day when they called, the answering voice became weaker. Finally, there was no answer at all.

More than a hundred years have passed. Still, the mystery goes on. What happened to David Lang? People have come up with many ideas. Some believe he went into another dimension. Others think he was picked up by a UFO invisible to the human eye. But no one knows. No one really knows how or why David Lang walked into a field one day—and disappeared forever off the face of the earth.

Water from Nowhere

In 1972, nine-year-old Eugenio Rossi was taken to a hospital on the island of Sardinia. Doctors who examined the sick boy found that he had a problem with his liver.

Eugenio was taken to a ward, a hospital room containing many patients. Nurses put the boy to bed to await treatment. But shortly after he got into bed, an odd thing began to happen. Water started to flow up through the floor in the room.

"It was coming up everywhere," said a nurse. "It wasn't like some sort of ordinary leak. It was as though water was being squeezed out of all the floorboards."

Plumbers were called. They searched carefully, but there was nothing wrong with any of the pipes.

Meanwhile, one by one, the patients were taken out of the ward. Finally, Eugenio's turn came. As he was wheeled out of the room, the flooding stopped!

He was put into another ward. And almost as soon as he entered the new room, water began to seep up through the floor there, too!

The nurses quickly took him out. This time he was put

in a room by himself. The same thing began to happen. But at least now the flooding wasn't bothering other patients.

Doctors began treating the boy. A clean-up crew had to work around the clock. As the doctors took care of Eugenio, the workers endlessly mopped up the floor.

As the days passed, Eugenio started getting better. As he did, the flow of water slowed down. Finally, his liver problem was cured. The flooding stopped completely.

It seems there was a connection between the boy's illness and the water that came up from nowhere. But what that connection might have been is anybody's guess.

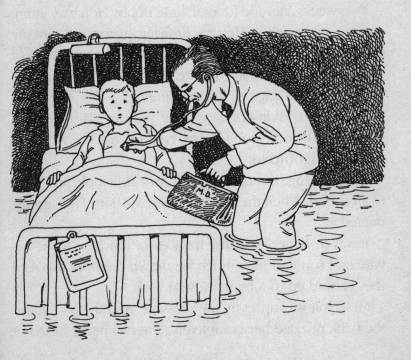

Message from the Grave?

Several years ago a North Carolina man, David Holt, passed away. His death was sudden and unexpected. His wife was left with almost no money and a four-year-old son to support.

Two weeks after the funeral, little Bobby Holt was sitting at the kitchen table. He was drawing pictures. Suddenly he pushed his drawings away. He took several sheets of clean paper and began to write. After filling three pages, he gave the message to his mother.

Mrs. Holt couldn't believe what she saw. The message was in shorthand. Young Bobby couldn't read or write, let alone use shorthand!

Not knowing shorthand herself, Mrs. Holt took the sheets to an expert. When the message was read, Mrs. Holt almost fainted.

It was from her husband! It told how much he loved his wife and son and how much he *missed* them. It also said they should go to a bank in New York.

Mrs. Holt was upset by the message. And the part about the bank puzzled her completely. She had never heard of the bank. She could think of no reason why she should go there.

Still, she did what the message had told her to do. She and Bobby packed their things and took the train to New York.

At the bank, Mrs. Holt talked to the manager. He told her that her husband had rented a safety deposit box long ago.

The box was opened. In it was a little cash. More important, there was a life insurance policy worth thousands of dollars. Never again would the young widow have to worry about money!

A story such as this is hard to explain. Did young Bobby somehow receive a message from the grave? If not, then how could he suddenly start writing shorthand? How and why was he able to locate the insurance money—money that only a dead man knew about?

The Electric Lady

THE DATE: November, 1967. THE PLACE: A lawyer's office in Rosenheim, Germany.

Everyone was going crazy. The world was going crazy. No one in the office could believe what was going on.

It had started on the morning of November 3, a Monday. Suddenly a neon lighting tube fell to the floor and shattered. No one knew why it had come loose. Still, it didn't seem like anything of real importance. The tube was replaced and everyone went back to work.

The next day the same thing happened. Again the tube was replaced. A moment later it began unscrewing itself! And so did all the other neon tubes! The clerks stared in amazement as the tubes went around and around without being touched. Then they took cover as the tubes came crashing down.

An electrician was called. He decided something must be wrong with the neon lighting system. He took it out and replaced it with one that used ordinary bulbs. When he was done, he turned on the lights. The new system seemed to work fine. The electrician left. Again, everyone settled down to work.

An hour passed. Suddenly, one of the light bulbs burst with a loud pop. Then, one after the other, all the bulbs exploded!

Again, the electrician was called. He had no idea of what was wrong. He turned off all the light switches. He left, promising to come back in the morning.

No sooner was he out the door than all the switches started going wild. Over and over, they flipped on and off. And no one was touching them!

But that wasn't the only problem. Already the photo-copier was doing all sorts of odd things. Weird noises were coming from inside it. Then, without anyone touching it, it started up on its own. Suddenly, it broke down com-pletely. Photocopy fluid spurted out all over the floor.

The machine was unplugged. The spilled fluid was cleaned up. For a moment, everything seemed to have returned to normal. Even the light switches had stopped acting up.

That's when all the telephones in the office started ring-ing. Over and over, clerks answered the phones. But there was no one there! As soon as a phone was hung up, it would ring again.

The phones were taken off their hooks. That should have solved the problem. It didn't. The phones started dialing numbers by themselves!

At this point, there was nothing that could be done except close down the office.

The office manager called the power company. They checked every part of the electrical system. Nothing seemed to be wrong with it. There was nothing that could explain all the crazy things that had happened.

The manager also talked to the police. They thought someone was playing some kind of a trick. But how such a trick could be pulled off, they had no idea.

The police questioned all the people who worked at the office. All were very puzzled—and a little frightened—by what had happened.

A 19-year-old clerk named Ann-Marie seemed most frightened of all. She had just started working at the office—on Monday. The job was new to her. She had been

very nervous. Then all the strange things started happening, and she had gotten even more scared. Now, worst of all, she had to talk to the police.

She was very tense as she walked into the room where the policeman waited. He asked his first question. Suddenly, the lights in the room started going off and on! File cabinet drawers opened by themselves! In tears, Ann-Marie ran from the room.

Somehow, it had been this young lady who had been causing all the impossible happenings. No one knew why, and certainly not Ann-Marie.

Doctors examined her. They could find nothing wrong with her, nothing ordinary. But tests showed that her body seemed charged with electricity. The electric charges became very strong when she was nervous.

She was given pills to relax her. Then she was taken to her parents' home to rest. But even there, the same sort of strange things happened.

As the weeks passed, the odd happenings slowly stopped. Ann-Marie got another job. Her first day there, it all started up again. She quit the job a few hours after starting.

Ann-Marie and her parents moved to a new home. It had no electricity. Her life became quiet and peaceful.

There have been a few other people like Ann-Marie. These people also give off an electric charge. But never has the charge been so powerful or caused so many wild things to happen. Her case is the most ususual one on record.

The Floating Man

He was known as Joseph of Copertino. Joseph was an Italian priest who was later made a saint by the Catholic Church. If what most history books tell us of his life is true, Joseph was one of the strangest men who ever lived.

Let's start at the end, with Joseph's death in 1663. Shortly before he died, it is said, Joseph rose into the air. Then he floated from his bed to a nearby chapel!

That was the last time Joseph flew.

The first was in 1629. Joseph was in church praying. He went into a trance. Suddenly he let out a shriek and rose into the air. As others in the church stared in disbelief, he slowly drifted down the aisle with his hands outstretched. He landed atop the church altar. On his knees and still in a trance, he continued to pray.

In the years that followed, Joseph flew many more times.

Once he visited Rome to meet the Pope. Seeing the Pope seemed to fill Joseph with joy. He went into a trance and rose into the air. He stood suspended off the floor for several minutes. The Pope and others begged Joseph to come down. After he had, the Pope ordered that a written record be made of the seemingly impossible thing that had just happened.

Another time, Joseph went to the home of a sick man. While the ailing man looked on, Joseph floated around the room and prayed for his recovery.

Joseph was even able to lift others into the air. One time he grabbed a madman by the hair and rose high above the streets of the town with him. Fifteen minutes passed before the two returned to the ground. When they did, the madman was cured. There were dozens of onlookers. Many fainted at the sight of what they had seen.

Naturally, all that you have just read is hard to believe. But hundreds of people between the years 1629 and 1663 claimed they saw him do it. With their own eyes, they saw Joseph of Copertino fly.

A Dream Come True

The date was May 7, 1915. Marion Holbourne was sitting in an easy chair in her home in London, England. She dozed off and had a very strange dream.

She dreamed she was on a sinking ship. The vessel was listing badly. Lifeboats were being lowered. Smoke filled the air. Frightened passengers and crewmen rushed about everywhere.

In her dream, Mrs. Holbourne was standing on the upper deck of the ship. She was not worried about her own safety. She was worried about her husband. He was a passenger on the ship, and she couldn't find him.

She spotted an officer, a young man with blond hair and brown eyes. She went up to him and asked about her husband.

The officer in the dream told Mrs. Holbourne that her husband was safe. "He's alive and well," said the officer. "I found him and helped him into a lifeboat."

With that, Mrs. Holbourne suddenly awoke. The dream frightened her terribly, for her husband at the moment actually was traveling at sea. He was on a British passenger liner called the *Lusitania*.

Upset, Mrs. Holbourne told her dream to her family. They laughed it off. "Just a silly nightmare," they told her. "Nothing to worry about."

A few hours later their views quickly changed. News came that the *Lusitania* had been torpedoed by a German submarine. Nearly 1,200 people had perished in the sinking.

But not Mr. Holbourne. One of the lucky survivors, he returned home to his wife and family.

"I owe my life to a young officer," said Mr. Holbourne. "For a while there I was sure I was going to die. The ship was sinking fast. There was smoke everywhere. But then this officer came to my rescue. He got me to a lifeboat just before the ship went down."

Mrs. Holbourne went pale as a ghost. "What did he look like?" she asked. "Do you remember?"

"Never forget him. A nice young bloke. Had blond hair and brown eyes."

Mrs. Holbourne was speechless. Her dream, down to the last detail, had come true.

Coming Home

This is one of the strangest stories you will ever read. It is the story of the life and death of Charles Coghlan.

Charles Coghlan was born in 1841 on Prince Edward Island. The island is off the coast of Canada. Charles came from a poor family. They did not have enough money to send him to college. But Charles was very bright and well-liked. Neighbors of the Coghlans took up a collection. With the money, Charles was sent to a college in England. He graduated with honors.

Charles returned home. He told his family he wanted to become an actor. His parents were very much against the idea. They said he was not cut out to be an actor. They told him to put such a foolish idea out of his head. And if he did not, they would have nothing to do with him. He would no longer be part of the family.

Charles and his parents argued. Neither side would budge. Finally, Charles decided to leave home. He told his parents they were terribly unfair. He told them that some-day he would return to Prince Edward Island. And when he did he would be a famous actor.

At first, it seemed to Charles that maybe his parents had been right. He traveled from town to town in Canada. He did get a few jobs acting in plays, but they were always very small parts.

After several years, he headed south, to the United States. There, his career began to take off. He started getting bigger and better parts. Eventually he was playing the leading role in important plays in cities all across the country. Charles' dream was coming true. Through hard work, he was becoming a rich and famous actor.

One day Charles visited a gypsy fortune-teller. She told him that he would die at the height of his fame. His death would be swift. Also, she said, it would happen in an American southern city. He would be buried there. Still, he would have no rest until he returned to the place of his birth, Prince Edward Island.

The fortune-teller's words bothered Charles. He often told his friends what she had said.

The years passed. Charles Coghlan's fame grew. People came from all over to see him perform. He was thought of as one of the most brilliant actors of his time.

In 1898, he was playing Hamlet in a southern city, Galveston, Texas. One night he suddenly grabbed at his chest. He took a few steps. Then he collapsed on stage. Other actors and people from the audience rushed to help him. But there was nothing they could do. Charles Coghlan, age 57, was dead of a heart attack.

He was buried in the Galveston cemetery.

Two years later a great hurricane roared through the

South. Galveston was especially hard-hit. Buildings were torn to pieces. Ships and boats were sunk. Much of the city was flooded.

Even the Galveston cemetery was not spared. Great waves pounded it. Bodies and coffins by the hundreds were swept away.

The storm finally passed. Friends of Charles Coghlan searched the ruined cemetery. His grave had been washed away. Not a trace of it or his coffin could be found.

In October, 1908, eight years after the hurricane, some fishermen on Prince Edward Island spotted a large box. It was floating in shallow water. The box was old and covered with moss and barnacles. The fishermen waded out to the box. They dragged it ashore and pried it open. In the box was a coffin, and in the coffin was the body of Charles Coghlan!

Somehow, it had all happened. Charles Coghlan had become a famous actor. Later, as the fortune-teller had said he would, he had died at the height of his fame in a southern city. Then he had returned home. In his coffin, he had traveled three thousand miles from the place he had been buried.

Charles Coghlan—brought home by the sea—was finally laid to rest on Prince Edward Island. The cemetery was beside the church he had attended as a little boy.

All in Sport

Football Game Won by Unconscious Player

It was November of 1923. The Texas Christian University freshman team was playing Terrell Prep. TCU beat Terrell by a score of 63–0. However, they would have lost if they had not had the help of an unconscious player.

TCU had only 20 players on its team. By the fourth quarter many of them had been injured. Finally, with only a couple of minutes left in the game, the coach looked around for a substitute. But there was no one left to send in!

TCU had only ten men on the field, but the rules say there must be eleven. The referees told the TCU coach that his team would forfeit the game unless they had the right number of players.

Just then, Ernest Lowry, who had been hurt on the opening kickoff, struggled up off a blanket and said, "I'm all right, coach. I'll go in." But the effort to sit up was too much for the boy and he passed out.

Suddenly, the frantic coach had an idea. He placed Lowry's blanket on the field just inbounds, and the unconscious boy was laid on it. He was far away from any action, but he was a legal eleventh man.

"We were on defense," the coach explained, "so Lowry could be any place back of the line of scrimmage. And he lay there during the final plays of the game. He gave us our eleventh man. It's the only time an unconscious player ever won a football game."

Fair Trade

Istvan Gaal wasn't a great soccer player. He wasn't even average. He was terrible.

He was so bad he was traded to a rival team for a *soccer ball*!

Gaal was a 21-year-old Hungarian. In 1970, he moved to Canada. He bragged that he had been a star back in his native land. He had, he claimed, scored 31 goals in 44 games one season.

Everybody in the Canadian Soccer League wanted this promising young star. The Concordia Kickers signed him. And then they wondered what they had gotten.

"We didn't know what to make of him," said John Fisher, president of the Kickers. "He had a few moves, but he looked lousy. At first we thought he was holding back. He had just come to a new country and couldn't speak the language. We thought he'd be okay once he got used to everything. But he never improved."

Gaal wasn't on the starting team of the Kickers. He couldn't even make it as a substitute.

During a game, Fisher was talking with the owner of the

Toronto team. Recalled Fisher: "He said, 'The kid's bad, but maybe I can do something with him. Why don't you just release him to me?' I said, 'No, I'm not just going to *give* him to you. I want something out of the deal.'"

The Toronto owner smiled—and offered a soccer ball in exchange. Fisher quickly accepted.

"It was a good trade," said Fisher. "They got what they wanted, and I got a soccer ball. They go for $27.50, which is more than the guy was worth.

"The trade actually wasn't all that unusual," added Fisher. "I went checking through the records. I found that a hockey player was once traded for a pair of nets."

Five on One

No basketball game has even been more unbelievable than that played in 1982 between Cal-Santa Cruz and West Coast Christian. In the game, five players took on a "team" of one—and lost!

Midway through the second half, West Coast was leading Santa Cruz by 15 points. Then they got into serious foul trouble. One after the other, West Coast players fouled out. Because of injuries, the team had only suited up eight players. When a fourth player was whistled out of the game, they could put only four men on the floor.

Still, West Coast held on to its lead.

But again and again the referee blew his whistle. Out went three more West Coast players. With 2:10 left to play, the team was down to one man: Mike Lockhart, a 6-foot, 1-inch guard.

According to the rules, a game can continue when a team has only one player left—if that team is leading.

When Lockhart found himself alone on the floor, West Coast was ahead 70–57. "I was really scared," he said. "I could dribble the ball, but there was nobody to pass to.

Also, I had four fouls myself, and one more and the game would be over. The worst part was inbounding the ball. The ref said I could only inbound it by having it touch a player on the other team."

Lockhart inbounded the ball by bouncing it off the leg of an opponent. Dribbling, weaving around all over the court, he ate up as much time as possible. Finally, he had to shoot. He missed, but managed to get his own rebound. Then he continued dribbling.

The Santa Cruz players couldn't believe what one man was doing to them. Frustrated, they kept grabbing at the ball, and fouled Lockhart—three separate times. Lockhart sank five of six free throws.

Almost every time Santa Cruz got the ball, they made a mistake. One player was called for traveling. Another missed an easy shot. Twice, in passing the ball, they threw it out of bounds.

Despite the fact they were playing five-on-one basketball, Santa Cruz scored only ten points. Lockhart scored five. The one-man basketball team held on to win, 75–67.

Best Catch Ever

Tom Deal loved to play softball. A Saturday in the summer of 1981 found him playing the outfield for a local Chicago team. His team was ahead, and all they needed was one more out to win the game.

He watched as the pitcher streaked in a fastball. A solid *whap*, and a towering fly ball looped out toward Tom. It should have been an easy catch. But Tom flubbed it. The ball bounced off his glove.

The other team went on to score five runs and win the game. Tom felt sick. His team had lost, all because he had missed a very easy catch.

That night he fell asleep, still brooding about the ball he'd flubbed.

He awoke the next morning to the sound of a baby crying. Tom looked out the window of his apartment. Across the way was another apartment building. And out on a third-floor balcony was a months'-old baby. To Tom's horror, he could see that the baby was crawling toward the open railing of the balcony!

Tom threw on a robe and dashed downstairs and across

to the other apartment building. Frantic, he rang the door buzzer again and again. There was no answer. But high above he could still hear the crying baby.

He looked up. His heart stood still. The baby was *through* the railing! Then it was falling, plunging three stories—to its death.

There was no time to think, just to act. The baby tumbled head-over-heels down through the air. Arms outstretched, Tom dove. And made an impossible catch!

The toddler was unharmed.

For a long moment Tom sat on the pavement, holding the baby, hugging it. He grinned from ear-to-ear. Yesterday he had missed an easy catch, one that had lost a silly game. Now he had just made an unbelievable catch—and had saved a human life.

Karate Team Knocks House Down

It was an interesting thing to watch. On a cold day in England not long ago, fifteen karate experts approached an old house. Then, using their hands, heads, and feet, they smashed the building to bits.

The six-room house was 150 years old and was due to be torn down anyway.

The team did not do the job just for fun. They did it to raise money for charity.

"It was a well-built house," said team leader Phil Milner. "It was a real challenge."

"The only hard part was the fireplace," said another member of the group. "It was made of about three tons of brick and cement."

The team, working in bare feet and karate suits, took six hours to destroy the place.

When it was all over, they bowed to the pile of rubble that had once been a house. Bowing to a defeated enemy is the final part of karate ceremony.

His Own Worst Enemy

Henry Wallitsch is not well-known to boxing fans. He should be; he did something no other boxer has done in the history of the sport. In a match held in New York in 1959, he threw a wild and crazy punch—*and knocked himself out.*

When the bell rang starting the fight, Wallitsch was really ready. He was up against Bartolo Soni. Soni had beaten him six weeks earlier. Wallitsch wanted revenge.

He came out swinging. Not Soni. He kept hopping around and dancing away.

Wallitsch got hopping mad. He kept flailing away—and missing. Some of the fans in the crowd of 1,500 were laughing.

Finally, Wallitsch got Soni in a clinch. And now had come his big chance. As he broke free, Wallitsch wound up to deliver the punch of a lifetime. With all his strength, he threw a mighty haymaker at Soni.

And missed everything.

The force of the missed punch carried him across the ring—and right through the ropes. He fell headfirst, and took one right on the chin, from the arena floor.

Looking over the ropes, the ref counted out the unconscious Wallitsch. Then he raised Soni's right arm in a signal of victory.

Even though Soni never really landed a single punch, the record books show that he kayoed his opponent. But that's not quite fair. It's Wallitsch who threw the winning punch—even if it was himself he knocked out.

Skier in Hot Water

Robert Rayor had been out for an afternoon of cross-country skiing through Colorado mountains. Suddenly, a snowbank gave way and he fell into an icy creek.

Rayor's wet clothes soon froze solid. He knew that if he tried to hike back to town he'd soon freeze to death.

Then an idea came to Rayor. He knew that not far away was a hot spring. It was his only hope.

Rayor hiked the short distance to the hot springs pool, took off all his clothes, and jumped in. The water was a comfortable 100 degrees.

For three days Rayor sat in the water, waiting to be rescued. Every so often he would drift off to sleep. But as soon as his head dropped underwater, he would immediately wake up.

Finally, Rayor was spotted by a rescue helicopter. The pilot dropped a backpack that contained food and clothing.

Rayor felt good. He assumed that the helicopter would be back shortly to rescue him. Then he noticed a note tied to a flare lying in the snow. Apparently, it had been knocked loose from the rest of the pack.

The note said that if he were Robert Rayor he should shoot off the flare. Since he hadn't done that, Rayor knew the helicopter would not return.

Rayor spent another night in the hot pool. The next morning he dried off as well as he could, put on the dry clothing the helicopter had dropped, and skied to a hospital.

All in all, Rayor was okay. Doctors found that he was suffering only from minor frostbite. They also found that he was very clean and his skin was wrinkled from the unusually long bath he had taken.

Weird
Weather

Have You Ever Seen a Frozen Breath?

In Siberia, it is not uncommon to have temperatures of 50 degrees below zero. One day in 1901, however, the temperature plunged to 90 below!

People had to wear masks, or some sort of air-warming device, over their faces when they went outside. If they didn't, their breath would freeze in the air and fall to the ground! When the frozen breath hit the ground, it made a soft tinkling sound and shattered into tiny pieces.

Breathing out was fun to watch. But breathing in could kill. If a person were to inhale without a mask on, his or her lungs would be instantly coated with frost.

Human Hailstones

It happened in 1930. Five men aboard a glider ran into bad weather. Their glider was lurching up and down. Ice coated the wings. Large hailstones were battering the craft to bits.

The five men decided to bail out. They checked their parachutes. Then one after the other, they jumped from the damaged craft.

For several seconds the men went into a free fall. They popped open their chutes. They continued their descent. All seemed to be going well.

Suddenly, a violent updraft lifted the men to the top of a cloud. There, they were coated with ice. Then they again began to fall. Down they drifted. Then another updraft caught hold of them. They soared skyward. They took on a second coating of ice, then again began to fall.

Over and over, the same thing happened. The men would descend. Then an air current would shoot them back up through the clouds. The coating of ice on their bodies became thicker and thicker.

The men may not have realized that they were going

through the same process that turns a raindrop into a hailstone. A raindrop loops up and down, gathering a layer of ice each time. When it is heavy enough, it falls.

Finally, the men were covered with ice. Each was a heavy ball of the stuff. In their parachutes, they dropped toward the earth. Like huge human hailstones, they swung back and forth on the ends of their lines.

When they hit the ground, the ice coating them shattered. All of them lay injured and in pain, and wondering at the amazing thing that had happened to them.

A Little Heat Wave!

On July 6, 1949, a freak heat wave hit central Portugal. The temperature rocketed up to 158 degrees! Not only is this the highest temperature ever recorded in that country, it is the highest anywhere in the world.

The heat wave lasted for only two minutes. Moments later, the mercury shot down to 120 degrees.

Many scientists have studied this strange, short heat wave. So far, they've been unable to come up with a satisfactory explanation as to how or why it happened.

Rain Out of a Clear Blue Sky

One day in 1958, Mrs. R. Babington returned home from an errand. She parked her car and started walking toward the back door of her house.

Suddenly it began to rain.

As she ran for cover, Mrs. Babington realized something was wrong. She stopped and looked up. Through the rain she could see the sun shining. There wasn't a single cloud in the sky!

At first Mrs. Babington thought a pipe had burst somewhere. Or perhaps the wind was picking up spray from a lawn sprinkler.

She began walking around her house, searching for the answer. But nowhere could she find a reason for the cloudless downpour.

When she walked out into the street, she realized the strangest thing of all. It was raining on her house, but nowhere else!

Soon, people began to gather in the street. They could see that rain was falling from the sky, but there were no clouds. And the rain was falling only in an area about 100 feet square.

For two and a half hours the water streamed down. Then, as suddenly as it had begun, the downpour stopped.

So far, no one has been able to explain the mystery. How is it possible for there to have been such a rain?